FRANCIS BOLA AKIN-JOHN

GROW THE
PASTOR
GROW THE
CHURCH

No Church will ever rise higher than the life of the Pastor

Grow The Pastor, Grow The Church

ISBN 978-372-9764

copyright (c) Dr. Francis Bola Akin-John

First Print   - 2005
Second Print - 2007

All rights reserved. No part may be reproduced without the written permission of the publisher.

All Scripture quotations are from King James version of the Bible, unless otherwise stated.

Published by:

CHURCH GROWTH SERVICES INC.

332, Abeokuta Expresswy, By Super Bus Stop, Oke-Odo, Agege, Lagos
Tel.: 234-01-8976100, 08023000714, 08029744296, 08054111301
E-mail: akingrow@yahoo.com   www: churchgrowthafrica.org

International Church Growth Ministries is an international and interdenominational ministry that is committed to supporting pastors and strengthening churches with resources and information for lasting growth. You can contact us at the address on this page.

Printed in Nigeria by:
LIFE & MINISTRY PUBLICATIONS
Tel.: 234-1-7934133, (0)8037152451

Dedication

Dedicated to
Pastor Joel Iyiola
of Bible Based Church, Ibadan,
for your wonderful pastoral
and leadership graces.

Dedication

Appreciation

It is of utmost importance to be appreciative. There are so many people who have been of immense help and support in the production of this book.

First and foremost, I give trillions of praise, honour, adoration, thanksgiving and glory to the Father of wisdom, His Son, Jesus Christ and His wonderful and marvellous Spirit, for the inspiration and illumination to re-write this book.

Secondly, my profound appreciation goes to those Pastors who have enrolled in our Church Growth School: International Institute of Church Growth, for deeper study in this wonderful and interesting subject; Church Growth. Your lives, faith and practise of Church Growth principles have been a source of inspiration to me.

My appreciation equally goes to the staffs of the ministry, Rev. Mike Oluwaniyi, Rev. Mike Olalere, Pastor Wale Olaoluwa, Bisola Erinfolami and Evang. Adedeji Adekusibe for their dedication and commitment.

May the good Lord bless you mightily. Amen.

Appreciation

Contents

Dedication	iii
Appreciation	v
Foreword to this New Edition	ix
Introduction	11
1. The Place of the Pastor in the Church	17
2. Pastor's Passions About Church Growth	33
3. Pastor's Myths About Church Growth	53
4. Personality of the Church Growth Pastor	67
5. Pastoral Mirror	87
6. Healthy Pastoral Leadership	109
7. Pastor's Personal Growth	127
8. Pastor's Price for Church Growth	147
9. The Pastor And His Co-workers	167
10. Alphabets of Achievement	191

Contents

Foreword To This New Edition

I have a great passion borne out of concern for Pastors and Church Leaders. I do not count myself to be wiser than many others who have already written to Pastors, but my calling and years of exposure have given me a passion for Pastors.

In the last eleven years, I have spoken to an annual average of 15,000 Pastors, usually in conferences, and also through other media resources, because I love being with and caring for these **"Called ones"**. Pastors and other spiritual leaders top my priority list for ministry, time and personal investment.

Check this sober Statistics:

Of the over 250,000 churches in Nigeria:
75% are sick and diseased.
15% are moving toward sickness
10% are healthy and growing

Of the over 30,000 Pastors in Nigeria:

10% know why churches are sick.
90% are inadequately trained.
70% are confused
50% are often depressed and discouraged
Yet over 80% work more than 60 hours a week, and there's no growth.

This book is borne out of a clear leading of the Lord to provide a bench-mark resource to Pastors and Church Leaders of today.

Too many things have gone wrong with pastoral ministry today which needs a clear voice. There is Pastoral crisis in today's church. The sad condition of the church is the direct result of uncooked, half-baked and immature Pastors being installed over churches. This new edition has been enlarged, more chapters added and explanation provided, in order for the church of today to be healthy through strong and healthy Pastoral leadership.

Today matters! We must forget yesterday, prepare well today so that we can have a good grasp of tomorrow. So I have a heart of concern, desiring to stand with those who struggle, warn those in jeopardy and encourage those enroute to victory.

Young Pastors will find this book illuminating and those who are training emerging Pastors will find the issues addressed helpful.

It is a sin to remain good when we can become better. Becoming a better Pastor is the focus of this revised book.

Dr. Francis Bola Akin - John.

Introduction

This new book, 'Grow the Pastor, Grow the Church' is the revised and updated edition of the old. The first one had been of tremendous success with Pastors. The comments, testimonies, observations and new information available necessitate the re-writing of the book.

The necessity and importance of this book cannot be over-emphasised. Much of the literatures available on Church Growth have not sufficiently stressed the importance of the Pastor to the growth of the church.

In Nigeria, nay Africa, it is largely taken for granted that the Pastor has little or nothing to contribute to the growth of the church.

However, one premise that runs through this book is that the Pastor is the number one key to the growth of the church. The word: 'Pastor' has different meanings to very many churches and denominations. But it is used throughout in this book referring mainly to people, (men or women) who are leading, directing, guiding and incharge of local assembly of believers, fellowships, chapels or congregations.

In the last twenty years, God has deemed it fit to bless the church in Nigeria and Africa with much growth, increase and expansion. Several thousands of churches have sprung up and are springing up daily. Many large congregations of several hundreds and thousands of worshippers are dotting our cities and states. And the growth is continuing unabated.

However, these encouraging growth and church planting cannot continue for a long time if the churches are being led by the wrong type of Pastors. The perpetuation of the work demands that the right type of Pastors must be placed in these churches.

I am fully aware that many of my conclusions may not go down well with some denominational leaders, yet I have no choice. Until we all embrace the principle of placing genuine Pastors incharge of our churches, the revival fire might die out.

This book is my sincere and humble contribution in this area. My utmost desire is to see greater revival and church growth in Nigeria and the whole of Africa. My calling is to work for the continuous growth of the church in Nigeria, Africa and the whole World. I will be more than fulfilled when the churches are being led by the right type of Pastors.

Who is the church growth Pastor? How can he lead his church to growth? What is the relationship between his personal growth and that of his church? These and many other questions are answered in this book.

This is a book for every Denomination, Church Leader and General Overseer. Every Pastor that desires to see unlimited growth in his church needs this book.

I am more than convinced that the church is the hope of the world and her revival rests in the hands of her leaders.

Dr. Francis Bola Akin-John
Lagos - Nigeria
July, 2005.

Introduction

"The church is strong
because the Pastor is strong.
The church is holy
because the Pastor is holy.
The church is growing
because the Pastor is growing.
The church is forceful
because the Pastor is prayerful.
The church is weak
because the Pastor is weak.
The life of the Pastor penetrates,
percolates, permeates and
pervades the life and blood
of the church".

- Francis Bola Akin - John.

The Place Of The Pastor In The Church

1

> "The Pastor is the king in the church and you don't mess with his crown"
> - C. Peter Wagner.

Today every serious church, ministry, denomination and fellowship of the saints don't joke with the position and place of the Pastor. They have duly come to terms with the importance and necessity of the Pastor to the growth of the church.

However, it has not always been like that. For too long, the place, position and importance of the Pastor to the growth of the church have not really been recognized and stressed.

Many obstacles, hindrances and bobby-traps are placed on the ways of Pastors. They are fought, resisted and worked against by many church leaders.

And the result has been stagnation, decline and retrogression of such churches. Many denominations are declining because they are noted for impoverishing and suffering their Pastors.

One truth we must ever remember is this: The Pastor is not the church, but God has limited what He will do in the church to the person of the Pastor.

The life of the Pastor is the ceiling for the church. Hardly do you see a church that rises higher than the Pastor. To see growth and health in the church, church leaders must allow the Pastor to truly lead and the people must truly follow.

Church Growth teachings stress strongly the importance of the Pastor to the growth of the church. To lead the church to growth and for the church to remain healthy, strong and vibrant, the Pastor holds the key. No principle of church growth is as important as this.

The Pastor must want the church to grow and be willing to pay the price. It is a known fact, yet largely unacknowledged, that the state and condition of the church reflects who the Pastor is.

An interesting survey was carried out some years ago, in which the unchurched people were asked what would encourage them most to select a particular church. Their response showed that the highest factor by far is the Pastor.

The Pastor is substantially more important to those unbelievers than the denomination, the facilities, the friendliness, the church programmes, the doctrines and even whether they have friends who go to the church or not. The Pastor therefore is the key consideration for the growth or non-growth of the church.

The first principle of church growth which states that the Pastor must want the church to grow and be willing to pay the price is a truism in many churches.

Even though there are places where the harvest is so ripe and God worked inspite of the Pastor and people, yet the future of such work and church is in jeopardy if the right type of Pastors are not available. I am going to expatiate more as we go on in this book but suffice to say now that not many Pastors want their church to grow.

Shocking but truthful! Many are satisfied with what they have already. Many are afraid of growth, while some are afraid of the hard work it would demand. Some are simply ignorant of how to bring growth to their church.

> Pastors are Christ's gift to the church and are responsible for the overall well-being of the flock

Another dilemma is that those who want their church to grow are not willing to pay the price. They consider the demands for growth as too stringent and thereby would rather let things remain as they are. These are things that contribute greatly to the non-growth of churches.

Now, let us look at the Biblical foundation for this all important issue:

BIBLICAL FOUNDATION

"And He gave some... Pastors..." (Eph. 4:11)
The ministry of the Pastor is one of the five-fold leadership gifts in the church. The word "Pastor" may be used in a very broad sense and yet it may also be seen in another angle to mean those ministry gifts that operate mainly as a pastor or a shepherd.

Christ is the Apostle, Prophet, Evangelist, Pastor and Teacher. All offices and ministries are in Him. Yet He has but one heart pulsating in all - that is, a Shepherd's heart. Therefore, all ministries, regardless of calling and placement in the body should have and be motivated by the heart of a Shepherd.

In that case, we may say that the five-fold ministries are "shepherding ministries". They all care for the flock of God. However, when Christ ascended on high, He gave gifts to men, ***"and he gave some... Pastors"***

All pastors are not apostles, prophets, evangelists or teachers. There are some people who have distinct pastoral call different from, yet related to the other four of the five-fold ministry gifts.

Christ continues His pastoral ministry in some persons distinctly called Pastors. Pastors are Christ's gift to the church. They physically represent Christ and are responsible for the overall well-being of the flock.

Some Greek words such as "piomen" "poimaino" and "Bosko" translated as pastor or shepherd, literally means that the Pastor is one who tends, guards, feeds, rules and oversees the flocks of God. (John 10:16; 21:16; I Pet. 5: 2, 3; Psa. 23:1-6).

It is important to understand the concept of the pastoral ministry in the Scriptures because it illustrates what God intended to manifest in the church.

The New Testament speaks of Christ as the Chief Shepherd and the elders / pastors as undershepherds of the flock of God (I Pet. 5:1-5; 2:25). Christ is indeed the Chief Shepherd of God's sheep. Many scriptures attest to this fact as noted in the following list:

1. The Lord is our Shepherd (Isa. 40:9-11; Psa. 23:1; 68:7; Zech. 13:7). It reveals His Divinity.
2. The Shepherd of Israel dwelling between the Cherubims (Psa. 80:1; 99:1)
3. The Man that is my Shepherd (Zech. 1:3-7) This reveals the Humanity of Christ by virtue of the incarnation.
4. The Shepherd stone of Israel (Gen. 49:24)
5. The Shepherd (Isa. 40:11; Jer. 1:10; Ezek. 34:23).
6. The One Shepherd (Eccl. 12:11; Ezek. 34:25).
7. The Good Shepherd (Jn. 10:10)
8. The Great Shepherd (Heb. 13:20).
9. The Chief Shepherd (I Pet. 5:4)
10. The Shepherd and Bishop of our souls (I Pet. 2:25).

The Lord Jesus Christ is our Pastor, our Shepherd and our Feeder. He is Jehovah - Raah *"The Lord is my Shepherd"* (Ps. 23:1). He became the pattern shepherd to all who are called to the ministry. It is His redemptive ministry to and for the sheep of His pasture.

> No one can function effectively in the pastoral ministry without a distinct calling and deep inner conviction from the Lord

Christ as the Chief Shepherd has many undershepherds throughout the world in His church, both universally and locally. There is but one church, one-fold, but many flocks of sheep. Christ gives as many sheep as we can handle. Thus, around the world there are flocks of many thousands of people, to hundreds, to fifties and to tens.

All Pastors in this sense, are but undershepherds, responsible for the flock of God and accountable to the Chief Shepherd. They are His sheep. The Pastor is to lead the sheep, guide and feed the sheep for Christ. To do that properly, he needs to truly be sure of his calling to the pastoral ministry.

PASTORAL CALLING

The word 'pastor' is one of the most bastardized word among churches and Christians in our nation. Every Dick, Tom and Harry now answer to it. Some people who only go for one week training come back to be ordained as Pastors.

Some denominations have thrown caution to the winds and any person that has 'connection' or can 'grease some palms' will be ordained as Pastors. Many who called themselves because they have failed in business, are among the lot. Many who also see the ministry as a commercial venture are now having a field day.

In some cases, ethnic consideration is used to determine who becomes a Pastor. In another situation, only well-to-do, educated and working class people are given preference when it comes to choosing and ordaining Pastors.

These practises are open secrets in many denominations and churches. Some Bible Schools and Theological Seminaries are equally causing much havoc by their arbitrary ordination of people. They failed to do sufficient and proper assessment of the people they are ordaining.

Many of those who are causing problems in the churches through breakaway are principally those ordained by these Bible Colleges. Furthermore, their churches are not growing because they have not been properly trained, monitored, groomed, scrutinized, tested and proved worthy.

A particular Bible School in Lagos takes the lead in this confusion. If Bible Schools are to ordain people at all, they must be those who have proved their ministry over a period of time with testimonies following and also based on the recommendation of the church or minister, under whose the ordainee has or is serving prior to his ordination.

Many churches are already reeking under the negative pressure of such wrong practises. And if we don't do anything to rectify such shameful and degrading practises, no matter how good our reasons for doing them may appear to be, the future will be bleak for the church.

No one can function effectively in the pastoral ministry without a distinct calling and deep inner conviction from the Lord. The pastoral ministry carry so much burden that it is only those who are called that can receive the grace to be successful.

The Pastor is directly responsible for the flock of God under his care and therefore will need a distinct "pastoral charisma" that will enable him to feed, gather, tend, care, heal and supply the needs of his flock, (Isa. 40:10-11). Even though the practise today is a far cry from Biblical standards, yet the

> People who should never come near church leadership are now posted to churches as Pastors

effectiveness of the pastoral ministry lies in the distinct call from God.

Many churches or flocks of God today lack genuine care, healing and supervision because of the neglect of this truth. Pastors are now chosen by vote, committee and appointed without due consultation with the Chief Shepherd, Christ Himself.

Many are in the pastoral ministry today who have no pastoral gift. People who should never come near church leadership are now posted to churches as Pastors. Small wonder then that such churches don't grow.

Since it has been established that the pastoral ministry is directly responsible for the superintending of God's flock, it goes without saying then, that the condition of the flock depends on who the Pastor is.

If he is God-chosen and a true shepherd, he will search and seek out His sheep as a shepherd to his flock. He will deliver them in the cloudy and dark days. He will bring them to their own land, to feed and pasture. He will make them to lie down in green pastures. He will strengthen them when they are sick. He will also judge the fat and strong sheep who hurt each other. He will bring them into folds (local churches).

But if he is an hireling, a thief or a robber, the sheep will scatter and be in disarray. A thief is one who steals by craftiness and subtle means. His only purpose is to steal from the flock their wool.

This is true of many Pastors and churches today.

They are only interested in what they will get out of the people. The robbers also "fleeced" the sheep for what they could get out of them. The hireling is one who is paid to do a job. He has no real heart or call for the sheep. It is but a job to him and he gets paid for it. He will flee when the wolf comes. He will desert the sheep and the wolf will catch, scatter or devour them. These are real but sad situations of many churches today.

EXPECTATIONS OF THE PASTOR

Harold Lindsell, Editor of **Christianity Today Magazine** stated; "The average Pastor is a burdened man. Although painfully aware that his church should grow in membership, spiritual vitality, evangelistic outreach and outgoing service, he is often at a loss on what to do. He doesn't need more exhortation. He needs help". It is such help that we will try to provide in this book.

The people's expectations of their Pastor is sometimes larger than he can humanly manage. An article in **Christian Herald Magazine** gave the result of a survey of what the people expect of their Pastor.

One church said they expected their Pastor to spend 10% of his time in study and sermon preparation; 60% in visitation and counselling; 10% in social activities; 5% with his family and 60% in parish activities and administration. The grand total of their

> The Pastor is very crucial to why people are leaving the church and he is the reason why many are coming and staying

expectations was 145%, which is often the type of pressure a Pastor feels when he does not have definite priorities in his goals.

Overcoming these various pressures, however, can help the Pastor to mature and grow spiritually. Spiritual maturity is imperative if the Pastor is going to see growth in the church.

"He will purify the sons of Levi (the ministers) refining them like gold or silver so that they will do their work for God with pure hearts".

STAGGERING STATISTICS

* 1,500 Pastors leave the ministry each month due to moral failure, spiritual burnout or crisis in their churches.

* 1,200 New churches are planted each month, but over 2,000 churches will close down.

* 50% of Pastors are so discouraged that they would leave the ministry if they could, but they have no other way of making a living.

* 80% of Pastors and 84% of their spouses feel unqualified and discouraged in their roles.

* 70% of Pastors constantly fight depression.

* 80% of Seminary students who enter the ministry will leave within five years.

* 80% of Pastors spouses feel their spouses is overworked.

* 80% of adult children of Pastors have had to seek help for depression.

* 80% of Pastors said they are sick and tired of dealing with disgruntled Elders, Deacons, Board members and Associate Pastors.

* 40% of Pastors said they have had extramarital affairs.

* 50% of Pastors' marriages will end in divorce.

* 80% of Pastors' wives feel left out and unappreciated by church members.

PASTORS CAN MAKE OR MAR

The cry all over the world is for better, stronger

and effective Pastors. Great and growing churches are noted for those who have the "pastoral charisma" leading them. And God seemed pleased to bless such congregations with great and spectacular growth. The Pastor may not be the reason why people come to the church for the first time, but he will be the major factor whether they will come back or not.

The Pastor is very crucial to why people are leaving the church and he is the reason why many are coming and staying. The Pastor of a church attracts who he is to the church. If he is educated, he will attract the learned. If he is young, he will attract the young. And if he is elderly, he will definitely attract the elders. Usually, you don't see old people going in large numbers to churches being pastored by young persons and vice versa.

> The Pastor must be the leader in the church. He must be first among equals

His outlook and belief in life will greatly influence his church and his people. God has kind of limited His workings in the church to the type of person the Pastor is. It is a general principle, even though there are exceptions, that 80% of the church reflect who the Pastor is.

The church, like every other human organization needs good, strong and dynamic leadership. When such leadership is lacking in the

Pastor, growth will be non-existent. Strong, dynamic and effective must be the Pastor for growth to happen in the church.

PASTORAL AUTHORITY

Before the Pastor can lead the church to growth, he must attain a leadership position which gives him proper pastoral authority. In other words, the Pastor must be the leader in the church. He must be first among equals. Those supporting him should hold him in high esteem and regard.

In churches where the Pastor only holds the title and position while the real authority and leadership is with some "pioneers," or the "patriach" or "matriach", there can be no growth.

The pioneers - those who were in the church before the Pastor or those who serve as "Elders", Boards or Trustees must give the Pastor the necessary support if the church is to experience growth. They should realize that God rules His people through an appointed man, not through committees.

The "patriach" or "matriach" - an influential rich man or woman in the church should allow the Pastor to function as the true leader if growth must happen.

The Pastor must be allowed to lead, share his God-given vision, purpose, goals and programmes with the people and in turn must be given support for the church to move forward.

Churches that undermine the position and leadership of the Pastor are usually non - growing churches. This point is so important that I will have to expatiate further in later chapters.

When the Pastor has the pastoral authority to lead in the church, then he should be held responsible for the state of the church.

Studies on church growth and decline have always confirm the Pastor as the principal key. The church will move forward when the Pastor desires, works for and is ready to pay the price for growth. The next chapter will examine this fact in greater detail.

Pastor's Passions About Church Growth | 2

> "Pastor! You either lead them up
> or you lead them down"
> - *Francis Akin - John.*

It needs to be stated that not all Pastors can lead a church to growth. Some Pastors are too gentle, while some are too hard for church growth.

Some have not developed leadership qualities and communication ability. Others lacked the required good human relations that augur for peace and progress in the church. The 21st century church can only be led by tough and tender Pastors. There must be a balance between toughness and tenderness.

One of the costly mistakes that Denominational Executives and Church Leaders frequently make, is to think that every Pastor and minister could lead a particular church to growth.

In the light of this, Pastors are posted, transferred and installed in churches without sufficient research as to the capability of the said Pastor to lead the church to growth. Where a young, dynamic and educated Pastor is taken away from, an elderly, weak and half-educated Pastor will be posted to replace him. The decline and stagnation of many churches is linked to this kind of costly error.

The popular phrase by John Maxwell that "Everything rises and falls on leadership" holds true in the dynamic relationship between the Pastor and the growth of the church. The overriding passions of the Pastor is what will drive the church.

To truly understand what is driving the church, we need to look at what drives the Pastor. Every Pastor is driven by something. There is something within that gives direction to what the Pastor is doing and saying. The condition of the church cannot be divorced from what drives the Pastor.

Here are some passions that serve as the driving force in Pastors lives and are automatically transferred to the church:

A.   Tradition:

Some Pastors are being driven by tradition. They see the need to maintain the tradition of the church and church fathers. They believe that the old tradition laid down by the church leaders are more important than any other thing and therefore strive with all their might to preserve them.

Their teachings, messages, prayers and style of leading major mainly on keeping the tradition the church is noted for. They care less about any other thing. This is the consuming passion of their hearts. And the church will definitely remain a traditional church and will be ineffective in winning the people of this present generation.

B.   Doctrinal Purity:

Pastors who are passionate about doctrinal purity are many. They have a kind of believe that every other person is wrong and they are the ones with the correct doctrine.

Holiness churches are found largely in this set up. They hold tenaciously to the believe that small is beautiful, since it will retain much quality. They think that growth is akin to compromise and lowering the standard of holiness. They go against every other Christian and church that does not see things from their particular perspectives. These set of churches will remain largely small, sickly and stagnant.

At this junction let me say, without sounding controversial that holiness is

> Pastors that are unduly passionate about doctrine usually don't care so much about growth

the standard for everyone that wants to get to heaven (Heb. 12:14). But what many considered to be the criteria for holiness and qualification for heaven remains controversial. Divergent views on this matter are what the devil has used to polarise the church in our nation.

However, to major on doctrine and used that as an excuse for non-growth is not pleasing to the Lord (I Tim. 2:4). Pastors that are unduly passionate about doctrine usually don't care so much about growth. In real sense, they are afraid of church growth. They usually take consolation in the fact that "at least we are keeping the standard".

C.   Maintenance:

This is another passion of Pastors that is closely tied to the last one. It is being mainly concerned with maintaining those who are inside already. It is an often refrain of Pastors with such passion that "my main concern is how to maintain my present members and take them to heaven".

They believe that their main task in the church is to keep on maintaining the members that are already within the church. This will reflect in the type of teachings or programmes and messages being given in such churches.

When maintenance is the secret and burning passion of the Pastor, the church will catch the bug and will be maintenance oriented. The chances of growth and vitality will be very slim and stagnation and decline will set in. The growth of the church demands proper balance between maintenance and outreach.

D.   **Providence:**

Providence as the sovereign workings of God is a good thing, but when carried to the extreme often results in fallacy. Pastors that are passionate about the providence of God to the extent that they believe that He is the owner of the church and He will make it grow when He so desires usually don't see growth. The growth of the church is laid squarely upon God only. They believe that they should hold things with some loose hands and God will work when He seems pleased. Their refrain is that they are waiting for God to move, not realizing that God has moved quite long ago.

In churches where the passion of providence is running in the heart of the Pastor, boredom, coldness, tiredness and disillusionment will be the order of the day since little or no efforts is made towards the growth, health and well-being of the church.

E.   **Messiah Status:**

It is a known fact that many churches are "personality oriented". Personality oriented churches are where the Pastor is the Messiah and everything revolves around him and without him the church flounders.

He is the soul of the church. He is indispensable. No one can do the ministry of the church like him. He is the only one capable of teaching, preaching, praying, witnessing and singing. He leads and takes control of every service, do the praying, worship, collect the offering, do the announcements and even count the offering!

He does not believe in training workers. He has workers, but training and developing them is not his priority. He believes that they cannot function effectively as he is, therefore it is of no use investing time and resources on them.

To Pastors that are driven by this particular passion, the condition of their churches speak for them. The stagnation, non-committal, uninvolvement and inactive state of the members are the outcome of such passions. Those whose only passion is to lord themselves over God's people are the bane of the growth of their churches.

> There are thousands of Pastors whose only passion is merely doing a job and getting their pay

F. Vocation / Profession:

There are thousands of Pastors whose only passion is merely doing a job and getting their pay.

They see the ministry as a profession and they are being paid to do a job.

In churches being pastored by such people, the care and concern for growth, expansion and increase will be non-existent. They may be stagnant, declining and sick, yet the Pastor will show little or no concern. His main preoccupation is how to get his pay for the 'great' job he is doing.

Such Pastors consider faithfulness in the ministry as more important than success or growth. Their usual postulation is that "God has not called us to be successful but to be faithful". However, their churches do not reflect their "supposed faithfulness". The evidence on the ground is a confirmation that the church is moving with slow and snail speed, and gradually grinding to a halt.

G. Competition:

It is an incontestible fact that several Pastors are being driven by the passion of competition. They are in competition with the Jones and Jonesses. They do everything with the consciousness that they are running and competing with a particular neighbourhood church. Their programmes, teachings and activities are geared toward outshining the other church.

Driven by this passion for competition, the church usually miss God's plan, purpose and direction for ministry. Copying the particular ministry style, programme and activities of others is a common occurrence among many Pastors in Nigeria and it has done incalculable damage to the effectiveness, growth and outreach potential of their churches. Comparing ourselves with others is not always wise.

H.   Ignorance:

Many may be surprised to see ignorance as a passion that drives some Pastors and churches. But it is true and real. It is commonly found among Pastors that are half-educated and whose churches God has blessed to an extent to think that they don't need to learn again. They therefore do not see the need to learn and be informed, since according to them "God is blessing our church despite our lack of proper education".

Such passion for ignorance usually manifest in areas such as unwillingness to learn, attend seminars, conferences and undertaking self-development courses that could better enhance their ministerial effectiveness. And they give subtle promotion to this ignorance when they declare to their people that "too much learning is madness".

Such pastors and their unfortunate churches are found all over the world. The observed scenario goes something like this; the beginning is wonderful and growth is natural and supernatural until a certain level is attained and the uninformed leaders could not handle it anymore and the bubble will start to bust, until the movement becomes a relic and move into oblivion.

Ignorance on the part of leaders has ruined more churches than we would readily admit and accept. In churches where this ignorance is a subtle passion, the future of the work will be greatly jeopardized.

It has happened over and over again and it is still happening. Ignorance is the bane of church health and growth. When the church outgrows the leadership, the church will move into a dead end. The growth of the church will be retarded by the ignorance of the leadership.

> In churches where ignorance is a subtle passion, the future of the work will be greatly jeopardized

TYPES OF PASTORS

To further show the relationship between the person of the Pastor and the growth of the church. I shall proceed to describe the four polar personality types of Pastors, their characteristics and behaviour that could affect their church positively or negatively.

If pastors are divided up in percentages, these are the four broad spectrum they fall into. The following pyramid will show it clearly:

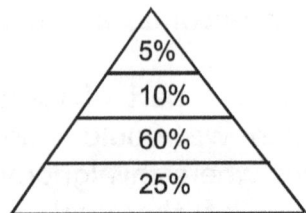

Characteristics and Behaviour of Pastors in the 25% range

1. Have synthetic self image
2. Critical of others
3. Can't admit own mistakes
4. Can't see others ideas
5. Preoccupies with himself
6. Believes he is self-sufficient
7. Uninterested in others
8. Unsure of his place in ministry
9. Negative and suspicious
10. Loves the crowd but hates the people
11. Inconsiderate
12. Defensive Tense.

Interpretation:

Pastors in this lowest range are usually in the ministry for what they will get. They are never interested in the health, growth or well-being of the church.

Churches with these range of Pastors are usually problematic and crisis ridden. They are stagnant and small. The Pastor is only interested in "fleecing" the people. He does not believe in growth. He sees the church basically as a means of feeding himself. They are in the lowest rung and are satisfied with little or no growth.

Characteristics and Behaviour of Pastors in the 60% range:

1. Have poor self image
2. Sensitive to real or implied criticism
3. Lack confidence
4. Don't understand self
5. Need approval of others.
6. Do not work by vision
7. Have no goal to pursue
8. Slow to learn from mistakes
9. Indecisive
10. Have low energy and drive
11. Have poor self-discipline
12. Content to float along
13. Maintenance oriented
14. Explain away lack of growth
15. Do not take responsibility for growth.
16. Complaining and critical
17. Celebrate average.

Interpretation:

Pastors in this range are a little better than those in the lowest range. However, their churches do not grow because their goal is just to make it through in life and ministry.

They constitute the largest percentage of Pastors in churches. Yet they see little or no growth. They sometimes desire growth but are not really bothered if it is not happening. They see their churches as the "faithful remnant". They remain small and non-growing because they are the only set of Christians maintaining the old time religion! They are largely maintenance oriented. Their major occupation is to maintain the saints inside the church.

Characteristics and Behaviour of Pastors in the 10% range:

1. Have good self-image.
2. Tolerant of others
3. Accept ideas from others.
4. Confident
5. Understand others
6. Desire to make impact
7. Not self satisfied
8. Comfortable with others
9. Have high energy and drive
10. Visionary
11. Train and motivate others
12. Positive
13. Flexible
14. Responsible.

Interpretation:

Pastors in this range are positive minded. They desire to win and want to be a winner in the ministry. They desire growth and are willing to learn and develop. They seek and desire effective ministry and ministrations. Even though great growth have not really come, yet they can make it happen. They are usually growth oriented. Which means they do everything with growth view. They have acquired church growth eyes and are willing to set the goals for growth.

Characteristics and Behaviour of Pastors in the 5% range:

1. Have good self image
2. Not sensitive to criticism but accepts it anyway.
3. Admit mistakes
4. Vision-driven
5. Communicates well
6. Confident
7. Understand self.
8. Persuasive
9. Calm and relaxed
10. Goal oriented
11. Patient
12. Growth oriented
13. Less need for approval
14. Can easily give approval
15. Learn from mistakes

16. Decisive
17. Understand people's motives
18. Confident
19. Have high energy and drive.
20. Positive
21. Self-disciplined.
22. Humble.

Interpretation:

This is the highest range, yet the most important set of Pastors. They are not many, yet they make things happen wherever they are found. Their churches are the great testimonies of their good, rich and effective leadership. They bring change and turn-around to otherwise barren, fruitless and declining churches. Their churches are not only growing, they are increasing and expanding. They are Pastors of today that God is using for the growth of His church. The most unfortunate thing is that Pastors with these qualities are in short supply. They are always hard to find.

From these percentages of Pastors, we could see that up to 85% of Pastors are not growth oriented. Only 10 percent are growth conscious and in actual sense, only 5%

> The desire to know God's plan for that particular church should be the number one driving passion of the Pastor

are seeing growth, increase and turn around in their churches and ministry.

Here we see abundant evidence that the growth of the church depend largely on the personality and the driving force of the Pastor. Pastors that desire growth must imbibe the right passions for growth to be seen.

If you find yourself on any range other than the highest one, you can move up by acquiring the right attitude and behaviour, then the prospect of growth in your church will be greatly enhanced.

PASSIONS THAT SHOULD DRIVE PASTORS

We have established that what drives the Pastor is what will drive the church. As the leader, so are the led. Now I want to examine what should be driving the Pastors if growth and health will be seen in the church.

God's Plan

The desire to know God's plan for that particular church should be the number one driving passion of the Pastor. Definitely, God has a plan and vision for every church. No two churches are the same. God has a plan and vision for each church. Until the church discovers God's plan for her in relation to her area of ministry, it will be largely ineffective.

God's vision for a particular church is unique. He plans to make every church effective in the community where it is situated. But lack of knowledge of God's plan for the church will hinder her growth and health.

By prayer, seeking God's face, meditation and study, the Pastor must find out God's heart-beat for the church. When this is the ruling passion in the Pastor's heart, growth is around the corner.

God's Purpose

The church was established by the Lord Jesus, (Matt. 16:18) so that it might be a shining light in a dark world. The church is also to defeat the kingdom of darkness in the community it is located. The church is a living organism which has one predominant quality; growth.

The purpose of the Lord for the church is to grow, increase and expand. (Acts 1:8). The Lord does not purpose a weak, non-growing, stagnant and powerless church. He desires a fruitful and effective church. He is glorified when growth, increase and expansion is happening. Growth is the goal and purpose of God for the church

"The righteous shall flourish like the palm tree: he shall grow like a cedar in Lebanon. Those that be planted in the house of the Lord shall flourish in the courts of our God. They shall still bring forth fruit in old age; they shall be fat and

flourishing". (Ps. 92:12-14).

Just as the palm tree, the church must experience all round and all season growth. Even in old age it must continue to grow and still bring forth fruit. When this purpose of the church has been discovered and embraced by the Pastor, growth will be natural and supernatural. When the purpose burns brightly as a passion in the Pastor's heart, the church is on the way to great things and places.

Great and growing churches in the world are being led by Pastors in the 5% range who believe and adhere strongly to growth as the purpose for the existence of the church. Nothing can dampen this strong passion for growth and their churches are the laudable testimony of this fact.

God's Command

The last words of our Lord Jesus was: **"Go ye therefore and teach all nations, baptizing them in the name of the Father and of the Son, and of the Holy Ghost, teaching them to observe all things whatsoever I have commanded you"** (Matt. 28:19-20).

This is the express command of Christ to the church. Obedience to this command should be the overwhelming passion of the Pastor. The church has no option than to obey.

Evangelizing and sharing the gospel, through various effective means should be the heart felt concern of every Pastor. When this is the case, the church cannot fail to grow and multiply. A going church is always a growing church. If we don't go we can't grow.

> Evangelizing and sharing the gospel, through various effective means should be the heart felt concern of every Pastor

Until the church begins to take this great command more seriously and seek effective ways of sharing the gospel, there will be no blessing from the Lord. When every other passion rules the heart of the Pastor in the absence of this one, the church will flounder, decay, decline and ultimately, die.

God's Glory

Bringing glory, honour and reverence to God should supersede anything in the life of the Pastor. Bringing glory to God in the church entails edifying, building and motivating the people.

Training and mobilizing the people for fruitful ministry in the church should be a passion on the part of the Pastor. Even though many Pastors are in the habit of doing everything in the church. They see the laity as people who cannot do the work of the ministry effectively since they are not "called".

The training and edification of the people must take a priority for growth to happen. The true meaning of Ephesians 4:11; that Pastors have been given, not to do ministry, but to train and develop the ordinary saints to do the work of the ministry must be imbibed. God is glorified when the people are trained to be effective in the ministry. God is honoured when everyone is using his or her God-given gifts for the growth and progress of the church. This must be a burning passion for the Pastor.

Until the Pastor jettisons the wrong passions and imbibe the right ones, growth will not be seen in the church to any appreciable degree.

The history of the church confirms that the church cannot rise higher than its leader. As it is with the Pastor, so also it is with the people. The church will only be effective to the degree the Pastor allows it. The passion that rules the heart of the Pastor is the one that will rule the church.

Pastor's Myth About Church Growth 3

"Your belief will either make or mar your growth"
- Francis Bola Akin - John.

Today, Pastors are awashed with various myths that have served to effectively hinder the growth of the church. Much theories have been expounded and postulations made in order to explain away why growth and vitality are lacking in most churches. Various reasons and strenuous attempts are often proffered to justify the non-growth, retardation and decline of the church.

These myths have now become presumptions, assumptions, theories and half-truths that Pastors, Leaders and Christians engage in when they want to quiet their screaming conscience.

Some of these myths are legendry in nature. They are embraced without proper scrutiny and appraisal. Strangely, God seems to limit His workings in the church to myths embraced by such churches. Myths serve as formidable barriers to church growth.

To fully understand these age-long myths, I will explain them one after the other and counter them with present reality and the truth of God's word.

MYTH 1

"It is okay not to grow. The small church is the perfect will of God".

REALITY

The church is a living organism which has life. And everything that has life must grow. The first Century church was a growing church (Acts 2:24-26).

Even though there are thousands of small churches that are in the will of God, yet growth is the goal of God for every church, either small or big. Moreover, the bigger churches have opportunity for ministry, outreach and missions more than the smaller churches.

MYTH 2

"God has not called us to be successful, He only called us to be faithful".

REALITY

Faithfulness and success seem to go hand in hand according to the story in Matthew 25:14-30. The first two servants were faithful in keeping their talents and successful in trading and gaining more. But the last servant was judged not because he was unfaithful in keeping the talent, but because he was unsuccessful in trading and gaining more.

When we are faithful, God is bound to reward us with success. No one can faithfully use his gifts in the right place and in the right way without being prospered by God.

MYTH 3

"Growth will happen without cause or effort by the church"

REALITY

Growth, sometimes is natural, but many times it is supernatural. It demands effort, prayers, toil and dedication. It will only come when we prepare, plan and work for it. Growth does not come suddenly when there has been no adequate preparation and plan for it. If it comes at all, it will quickly fizzle away.

MYTH 4

"Growth is akin to compromise. Growth tends to lower the standard of godliness in the church. The more quantity, the less quality of the life in the church".

REALITY

Church growth does not concentrate only on numerical increase of the church to the detriment of spiritual vitality. It holds both in proper balance. Quality and quantity growth go together.

Every church experiencing quality growth must experience quantity growth, else decay will set in. And every church experiencing quantity growth must also experience quality growth, else decline will set in. The truth is, you will get quality out of quantity. In other words the more quantity you can get the more quality you are bound to get too.

> No one can faithfully use his gifts in the right place and in the right way without being prospered by God

MYTH 5

"Growth is not happening to us because we are the faithful remnant. We are so holy and pure that the sinning world tends not to join us"

REALITY

Every church infected with this negative piety will languish and flounder. The church is not a selected club of few. It cannot be too holy not to affect her immediate environment. The messages cannot be harder than that of Jesus, yet He saw multitudes flocked in to hear Him. The church must function as a place where sinners will get born again. Every church that considers herself too holy to win sinners is not in the perfect will of God.

MYTH 6

"Providence will do everything. God is the author of growth and the owner of the church and He will make it grow when He wills".

REALITY

This pious statement has done much havoc to the growth and well-being of the church. The Scriptural position is that even though God can grow the church without us, yet He has decided not to. We have our part to play and He has His part to play (I Cor. 3:6-9). We must labour together with God for the onward growth of the church. Without us, God has decided not to do anything (Acts 8:26-38). When growth is desired and we are ready to pay the price for it to happen, then God will play His part by sending growth.

MYTH 7

"The most important thing is to maintain the saints that are inside and sinners will naturally be won to the Lord".

REALITY

The truth of the matter is that churches that believe and hold tenaciously to this myth are largely non-growing and stagnant. Concentrating on those who are inside will make the church inreach and not outreach oriented.

Maintenance oriented Pastors tend to have churches that are cold, lukewarm, bored and stationary. Without sufficient motivation, the saints will not win the sinners.

It needs to be stated that the saints will only remain alive, vibrant and lively in the faith when they actively engage in winning and bringing their neighbours, friends, colleagues and relations to the Lord.

> Every church that considers herself too holy to win sinners is not in the perfect will of God

Maintenance oriented

churches usually become a club and a small enclosed circle of people that will gradually, but nonetheless lose their first love, zeal, passion and will ultimately decay and die.

MYTH 8

"Vision is not really necessary to the growth of the church. What is necessary is the willingness to serve the Lord".

REALITY

Willingness and whole heartedness are prerequisites to serving the Lord, yet it is almost valueless without a clear, concise and definite vision from the Lord. There are many thousands who are serving the Lord whole-heartedly, but who have not received God's vision for their lives and churches. Such churches will remain barren and largely unfruitful in spite of much effort.

The place and importance of vision to the growth of the church cannot be over-emphasised. People commit themselves more to a vision than to a personality. A church without vision is like a wedding without the bride - missing the essential element.

There is a vision the Lord wants your church to follow and fulfil. It must be discovered and pursued. (Acts 13:1-3). It must be translated into practical, achievable, believable and concrete goals. Only then will the growth and progress of the church be open for all to see.

MYTH 9

"Dedication is all we need. When we could keep on praying, reading the Bible, living holy and faithful in witnessing, growth will naturally come".

REALITY

Mention could be made of thousands of Pastors who are doing all these and yet their churches are not growing. There are several thousands of godly, praying and faithful ministers, who however see little or no growth in their respective churches.

The principles that guide the well-being and growth of the church must be learned, imbibed and practised. Growth will come when the right principles are applied in conjunction with godly and strong leadership.

MYTH 10

"The present members of the church are the bane of the church. They are largely unserious, non-committal and inactive. If only they could change, the church will grow"

REALITY

One reoccurring problem in several churches is the issue of 'lethargic laity'. The members are uninvolved, non-committal and inactive. However, the minister is largely responsible for this problem.

It is a common practise among Pastors to blame the laity as the reason why the church is not growing. But the minister should be held responsible. He is the number one key to the growth of the church and when he does not share the vision, train the people, state his expectation from the people, give them the opportunity to partake and share the ministry, then the condition described above earlier will be the order of the day because the people will not contribute effectively to the growth of the church until they see change in the leadership and they are given the chance and encouragement to partake in the ministry.

> A church without vision is like a wedding without the bride - missing the essential element

MYTH 11

Pastors are not really important to the growth of the church. Therefore, they can be changed, transferred to any location, as long as they are ministers and the work will move on".

REALITY

This is one grave error that has destroyed many otherwise promising churches. God places much premium on the Pastor of a church. The growth or decline of the church centres on the Pastor. Church health, growth and dynamism is strongly tied to who the Pastor is. Research after research have confirmed this salient truth.

Denominational Executives have transferred Pastors without due regard and recognition of this fact thereby making decline inevitable. It needs to be reiterated again that, not every minister can successfully Pastor and lead the church to growth.

Ministers with core evangelistic gifts whether they are prophets, counsellors or administrators, will find it hard to lead a church to growth. They can maintain, but outright growth will be difficult due to obvious reasons. When such fact is not taken into consideration during the time of posting and transfer, much havoc will be done to the church.

Another equally damaging side to it is the failure to take the education standard, enlightenment, grace and capability of Pastors into considerations when posting is being done.

Pastors with high degree of education, dynamic gift, grace and capability will be removed and in his place, a Pastor with low level education, elderly and inexperienced will be brought in. It is a fact that the church will plateau, decline and decay for the simple reason of the vast difference in the person of the Pastors.

For the sake of church health and growth, Pastors of almost equal age, ability, education and capability should be exchanged when it is transfer and posting time.

MYTH 12

"Pastoral brevity. Pastors need not stay long in a place before growth will manifest".

REALITY

Church growth research has confirmed that pastoral longevity helps the growth of the church a lot. Pastors need to be in a church for at least four years before the bias for growth will begin to manifest. Short and brief period of pastoring does not leave enough room for growth programmes to be commenced and consummated.

Denominations that have the habit of transferring Pastors in two or three years interval will discover that such ministers would not make much lasting impression for growth in such places.

In actual fact, the first two years is usually for familiarization with the new environment. Growth plan and programmes will only begin to take root in the third year. The exception is when the incoming of the Pastor has brought serious decline, decay and boredom in the church. People will only support and make serious commitments when they realize that the Pastor will not be hastily transferred again to another branch or elsewhere.

> Short and brief period of pastoring does not leave enough room for growth programmes to be commenced and consummated

Church growth is becoming one of the cutting edge of studies in this end time. Many Christians who are committed to the fulfillment of the Great Commission are showing tremendous interest in the growth of their churches.

Today many previously non -Pentecostal and spiritual churches are now changing to Pentecostal churches. God is working mightily in this end time. However, many pastors and ministers who have learned and are familiar with church growth are yet, not growing.

They are still confused and bewildered as to how to lead their churches to growth. They still moan and lament the state and condition of their churches and this is because of the above mentioned prejudices and dogmatic beliefs. Until these dogmatic beliefs are removed and changed, growth might not be possible.

Until we shed all these garment of myths and

embrace the realities, growth will be a mirage. Church growth demands that we have the right approach and attitude toward growth as ministers.

The church cannot rise higher than the Pastor's belief. When the Pastor does not possess the attitude of growth, things will take a turn for the worse. 'It can be done attitude' is very important. If you are positive-minded and believe that you will see growth despite the discouraging circumstances, growth will surely come.

Personality Of The Church Growth Pastor — 4

> "You cannot lead any farther than you have gone yourself"
> - *Francis Bola Akin - John.*

In this chapter, the focus will be on the personality of the Pastor that will lead a church to growth. Moreover, we need to examine the type of Pastors that God will use to bring growth and vitality to the church.

In as much as the church will be permeated with the personality and lifestyle of the leader, we need to examine critically the type of leaders God seems pleased to bless with growth.

These personality traits came from years of research and observation of pastors and leaders who are experiencing growth in their churches. As with every rule, there will be exceptions. God reserved the right to use anyone for the growth and prosperity of His work.

However, the general rule is that Pastors and leaders whom God seems pleased to bless with growth have some certain characteristics and personality traits that greatly enhance the progress and prosperity of the task. But sadly, majority of Pastors do not possess the personality traits to lead a church to growth.

Therefore, I would first want to explain what Church Growth stands for before I proceed to describe the personality of the Church Growth Pastor.

IS CHURCH GROWTH RELEVANT TODAY?

Church Growth is a new study area that has received much criticism, misunderstanding, rejection and outright misrepresentation from those who should know better.

Many are contending that Church Growth teachings are not relevant to the situation the church has found herself today.

Well, Church Growth teachings centre around the fulfillment of the Great Commission of our Lord to the church. Church Growth teachings are infinitely concerned about the health, well-being and vibrancy of the church, and how the Great Commission is being carried out.

Church Growth covers eight major areas of growth in the church, namely:

- **Numerical Growth-** The church must increase numerically
- **Spiritual Growth** - Corresponding spiritual growth must happen.
- **Financial Growth** - Financial increase is part of all round growth.
- **Physical Growth** - The structures are important, the buildings are necessary.
- **Social Growth** - The church must have a good image in the community in order to make impact.
- **Material Growth** - The human and material resources to back up the growth are absolutely essential.
- **Extensional Growth** - New churches must be planted.
- **Health and well-being** - The church must not be sick.

These eight areas of church growth are essential to the overall well-being of the church. If any one is neglected, the church will flounder and remain imbalanced.

> A person with a world-wide vision will never be satisfied until he will build a big sanctuary of worship

Not many churches however, are doing enough in any of these eight areas, the more reason for the relevance of Church Growth teachings today.

Church growth is not only for small, struggling, sick and stagnant churches which litter the landscape around us today, they are also for growing and vibrant churches. And that leads us to the question, how big can a church become?

BIG OR SMALL CHURCHES?

The controversy has raged among Pastors and Church Leaders about how big or small a church can or should be. Are small churches the will of the Lord? Are big churches a curse? The arguments for and against big or small churches have raged on silently for many years.

Without necessarily sounding controversial, I would strive to present what I believe is a balanced answer here:

To the question; how big can or should a church be? I answer, your church is as big as your vision. Vision goes a long way to determine the bigness or smallness of a church.

Somebody with a small vision will undoubtedly be content with a small church. Likewise, a person with a world-wide vision will never be satisfied until he will build a big sanctuary of worship. Both small and big churches are in the will of God. God is pleased with some small churches and also at home with big churches.

DEFINING SMALL AND BIG CHURCHES

In this context, small churches are those churches that record an average of 100 people in attendance on a Sunday. While big churches are from 250 in attendance. Up to 85% of churches in Africa are in the category of small churches.

Big churches are also becoming a common site in the big cities and capitals of States in our Continent today. Both the small and big churches serve the purpose of God for this generation. They are both necessary and needed for this our time.

However, there are different characteristics displayed by the small or big churches. Below are some of them:

Small Churches	**Big Churches**
* Tucked in a corner in the Community	* Have greater presence in the community.
* Limited in finance	* Have more finance
* Limited in ministries	* Have more ministry Opportunities
* Have few manpower for Outreach.	* Have more manpower

* Limited opportunity to use gifts	*More room to use gifts and graces.
* Maintain deep fellowship together	* Bring more glory to the Lord through greater impact.
* Possess close knit family spirit with limited chances of reaching more people.	* Brings more respect to the gospel
* Largely inwardly focused	* Can reach and win more people.
* Create local-champions among members and hardly encourage discovery and development of ministries.	* Create rooms for members' ministries to be discovered and developed.

I should make bold to say that in some situations and localities, the small church is the perfect will of God. They are good and perfect example of God's love and power in some certain communities.

However, because of my strong believe in church growth, I believe that bigger churches are more "better" and preferable in most cities and towns of today than small churches.

This is not to say that Pastors of small churches should condemn and crucify themselves, but rather they should pray and seek out God's will for their churches, maybe the Lord desires it to be small or big.

My unshakable conviction is that the Lord wants every church to carry out the Great Commission, and if it is so, the church must be prepared to grow.

The Lord desires the growth of His church through the fulfillment of the Great Commission. Every church that takes the Great Commission seriously must grow because a going church is a growing church. (Matt. 28:19-20; Acts 1:8).

WHO IS THE CHURCH GROWTH PASTOR?

I should reiterate and emphasis that not all Pastors can lead a church to growth. Many Pastors are only good for small churches, their constitution is only suited to maintenance and non-growth.

They are okay with the small nature of the church and the close knit fellowship they enjoy with their members. They are satisfied with the usual round of visitation, prayer, counseling and help given and received from the church. They envisage spending the rest of their lives in that local and small church. They do not possess the required characteristics to either lead a church to growth or keep growth on course in the church.

I will now proceed to describe the personality traits of a Pastor that can bring growth to a church and keep that church on the trail of continuous growth.

1. **He is godly and exemplary in conduct:**

He is aware that his life is his ministry. He is not only born again, he is soundly saved. He is committed

> Church Growth Pastors the world over have always united on the need to maintain a deep personal life of prayer and communion with God

to personal godliness - pursuing holiness of heart and life. He does not believe in the saying "Do as I say, don't do as I do".

He knows that his life is being read and copied by his people more than anything else and therefore consciously determine to be exemplary both in life and conduct. He says more with the manner of his living than his words.

A powerful preaching is only backed up and made effective by right and godly living. He is deeply aware that his sermon only last some few minutes but his life preaches all through the week.

2. **He is deeply committed to personal prayer and communion with God:**

Church Growth Pastors the world over have always united on the need to maintain a deep personal life of prayer and communion with God. This is the most distinguished trait of a church growth Pastor. He spends time with God. He creates time to be alone with His God.

He does not allow anything to crowd out his time of communion with the Lord. He is early and late on his knees. He knows that his prayer life is the number one key to the growth of the ministry and that if he fails to maintain a regular, private and continuous time of prayer with the Lord, he cannot prosper in the ministry. He does not allow activities, business and meetings to hinder him from ministering to the Lord. Ministry to the Lord must ever come before ministry to the people.

3. **He receives his strength from the Lord:**

The Pastors that lead their churches to growth are men that realize that they cannot do anything with their human and natural strength. They therefore look up to God for strength and anointing. They don't joke with God's fresh infusion of anointing. They are aware that the anointing is what makes the difference in the ministry.

They know that if God does not work, nothing else will work. If the Spirit does not move, nothing else will move. They therefore wait upon the Lord continuously in order for them to minister in the strength of the Lord. They wait until the hand of the Lord will rest heavily upon them to give them supernatural strength, speed and success in the ministry.

4. **He is a man of vision and faith:**

Vision has been the distinguishing feature of Pastors of growing churches. They possess God-given vision. Vision of what God intends the church to do and where will burn brightly in the hearts of church growth Pastors. Their vision is what gives them focus, direction and motivation.

They are driven by a compelling vision of what they want to achieve for God and His church. They are a testimony to the fact that nothing great was ever achieved without vision.

These Pastors are never satisfied, they keep dreaming dreams of God. They know that the growth of their churches depend upon the dreams and vision they possessed.

They turn these dreams and vision into reality by making plans for goal attainment. They set practical goals in line with their vision. They pursue and work assiduously to attain the goals and the more reason their churches continue to grow and flourish.

Vision and goal setting are statements of faith. The faith of church growth Pastors is what God seems pleased with before blessing their churches with outstanding growth.

5. **He sees himself as one who is enrolled in life - long learning:**

A cursory look at Pastors of the World's largest churches will reveal that they are men who keep on learning. They are not narrow minded individuals who think they cannot learn from others. They are not arrogant people who think they know it all. They are eager to talk as well as listen and learn. They are men that have learnt to be eclectic - a borrower from every field that can help their ministries.

They attend seminars, conferences and take specialised courses on Church Growth which will help them to have a better grasp of their churches. Journals, magazines and good books are their constant companion because they have realized that the day they stop learning, they stop leading.

> Leaders are learners and church growth Pastors must especially learn in order to face up to the challenges of a growing church

Leaders are learners and church growth Pastors must especially learn in order to face up to the challenges of a growing church.

6. **He learns to delegate:**

Most Pastors don't delegate. They find it hard to train and release their people for ministry, but the Church Growth Pastor spends his time as a player-coach. He participates in the ministry but sees his primary responsibility as that of training and equipping others so that his ministry is multiplied. He trains people because he sees himself as a developer of people.

His people are free to use their God - given gifts

without let or hindrance, jealousy or envy. In fact, he opens doors of opportunities for people to use their gifts, talents and graces. He doesn't feel threatened by the gifts of his people. He rejoices when they move up in the ministry.

The Church Growth Pastor sets up training in the church in order to develop his people according to the God-given vision for the church. Periodical and systematic seminars are conducted to share, communicate and motivate the people towards joint effort in achieving the vision of the church.

7. He strives for better preparation and leadership:

The Pastor must know fully well that leadership is not position, title or name. But he must realise that leadership is influence - the ability of one person to influence others to accomplish a set objective and goal. The Church Growth Pastor must constantly strive to prepare himself for better leadership. Great growth is the result of good leadership and poor growth is the result of poor leadership.

Pastors of growing churches keep on digging for better character foundation and better preparation by the Lord so that they can continue to provide the right kind of leadership that will bring unlimited growth to the work at hand.

Continuous self-development is a marked feature of Pastors of growing churches. They keep on praying, studying, digging and preparing for better future.

8.   **He is deeply passionate about soul-winning:**

Pastors of growing churches are passionate people. They are deeply concerned about the perishing souls. The burden for the lost is a consummate passion for them. They also share this burden with their people such that the whole church becomes passionate about soul-winning. They believe too that more souls must be added to the church through outreaches.

> The love and concern for souls always result in many people being won to the Lord

The love and concern for souls always result in many people being won to the Lord. They therefore make use of every opportunity, resources and energy in their efforts to win more souls before the night comes.

9.   **He is not argumentative and narrow-minded:**

Growing churches in the world over are pastored by men who are broad-minded and flexible. They are not argumentative and narrow-minded men. They have seen God at work, both in their lives and in the lives of others and therefore are willing to accommodate the ways God may choose to work.

They have learnt to adapt and change methods, systems, styles and strategies that seem not to work to those that can bring results.

In reality, Church Growth Pastors are agents of change. They are willing to change old, archaic, traditional ways and methods that have gone with time to new ways that will appeal to people of this generation without compromising the scripture or its standards.

They realize the power and effect of change, and without compromising gospel truth, they are ready to effect necessary changes that will bring more effectiveness to the church.

10. He is an optimist:

Research have shown that church growth demands that the Pastor possesses an incurable optimistic spirit. A pessimist cannot grow or lead a church to growth. A negative, narrow-minded and impossibility - thinking person cannot lead a church to growth.

Growing churches are being led by Pastors that possess strong faith in God to do the impossible. They have confidence in God and also in their God-given abilities. They are not being worried by inferiority complex, and are not incensed by the seeming giftedness of fellow ministers. Rather they concentrate all their energy on being their self, and their best for the

Lord. They trust the Lord to fulfil His promise and bring breakthrough to the work.

The optimistic outlook of the Pastor definitely affects his people and they in turn are motivated to work for the growth of the church.

The above mentioned personality traits of Pastors of growing churches have been blessed by the Lord for the expansion of the work.

Pastors and church leaders that desire growth will do well to look them over and inculcate those lacking in them into their lives. Change should be effected where necessary and God in His infinite mercy will bless the church with great growth.

HABITS OF EFFECTIVE PASTORS

A habit is a practise, behaviour, pattern, routine, tendency, habitual action, fixed practise, or confirmed way of doing things. Habit can be servants, tools, helpers, or they can be rots that take us toward oblivion. Habits can be good or bad.

It is incumbent upon Pastors to cultivate habits that enhance ministry and character. Let's just take a

> Who you are shouts louder than what you say everytime, be plain, consistent, dependable and a person to be trusted and count on

look at the following bits of advice on habits accumulated from long years of ministry and from many sources.

1. Start every day with God: Bible reading, prayer and meditation.

2. Make a plan for each day: Set some immediate daily goals, short range goals, and long - range plans. Plan your work and work your plan.

3. Keep priorities in mind: God, yourself, your family and ministry.

4. Cultivate a habit of being punctual.

5. Determine to be a living example of what you preach.

6. Live within your means. Pay your bills on time and set aside a little for a rainy day.

7. Set aside time everyday for family needs. Plan special times with your spouse and children, away from the demands of day - to - day ministry. Cultivate a good family life.

8. Never step into the pulpit unprepared physically, mentally, spiritually or psychologically. Keep yourself fit in all these areas.

9. Do a brave thing - Physical exercises are essential to your physical health.

10. Become a student of the word, of good literature and of people.

11. Cultivate a positive mental attitude. Don't allow yourself to become angry, defensive, defeated, caustic or negative.

12. Be a peace maker, not trouble maker. Short tempers do not make for long ministries. A controversialist will make a bad Pastor.

13. Who you are shouts louder than what you say every time. Your life is your ministry. Be plain, consistent, dependable and a person to be trusted and count on. Be a person of integrity and honesty.

14. Read, read, and read more. Read a book a month and subscribe to periodicals.

15. Build your library diligently.

16. Keep a functional office. Your office is your growing, groaning and glowing room.

17. Learn to say nice and positive things. Never

speak ill of anybody publicly.

18. Deliver on your promises and don't make foolish promises. Have no secret dealings with anybody.

19. Be an enthusiastic, positive and a flexible person.

20. Never counsel anybody of the opposite sex alone or behind closed doors. Converse sparingly with women in private. It is foolish for you to think you shall not be tempted in such situations.

21. Take a day off each week; take your annual vacations.

22. Be a tither and a giver of offerings: be generous with everything you have.

23. Be loyal to your church, your church Board, your family, your God and your denomination. If you can't be loyal, get out; do something else.

24. Don't be a plagiarist. If you use other people's materials, give them credit. Don't be a taker only: put something back into the pipeline of ideas and concepts for others to use too.

25. Don't allow others to take your decisions for you. Be decisive. Stop facilitating.

26. Develop a good relational skill with people. Your mood and disposition will affect your ministry. How you relate, deal, care and get along with people will determine 80% of your ministry success.

27. Be accountable to a good and matured mentor and be willing to be under authority and discipline.

28. Be a good neighbour and be approachable. Treat everybody alike, from C. E. O to little children.

29. Don't become known as a long - winded preacher. Standup, speak up and shut up.

30. Cultivate a sense of humor. A preacher without a sense of humor is like a car without a bumper.

31. Keep working on your ministry skills and your sermon preparation. Work on your sermon delivery and your people skills. Become a lifelong learner. Continually upgrade yourself.

32. Get in the habit of never taking yourself too seriously, superiority complex is inexcusable in a

Pastor. Be willing to apologize and admit wrong. "If you mess up, "fees up.

33. Remember, your Board members are not the enemy, neither is your neighbouring Pastor or church.

34. Develop a hobby and leisure activities, but don't let any of them control and dominate you.

35. Just be nice! Remember who you are serving. It is always good to be good, because the pay is good. Forgive and forbear.

36. Remember to live each day at a time and to live with eternity in view.

37. Sow seed and invest in the life and ministry of others.

38. Be a developer and not a limiter of people. Your converts today are your future.

39. Make the Holy Spirit your senior partner. Without Him, you are nothing.

40. Ask for the prayers and intercessions of your people. Don't be too proud to request for prayers. Have intercessors to uphold you.

Pastoral Mirror 5

Pastoral gift is one of the five leadership gifts that is so much important to the health and well-being of the church according to the book of Ephesians 4:11.

The Pastor is not the church, but God has limited what He will do in the church to the person and character of the Pastor. Pastors are responsible for the growth, dynamism and direction of the church. A competent Pastor is the key to a contagious church.

Furthermore, a wrong Pastor is the first signal of a bleak future for any church. The moment the church has problem with who becomes the Pastor, downward spiral has begun in earnest.

To kill a vibrant church, you simply have to take the wrong Pastor there, and to revive a dead and stagnant church, you simply need to place the right Pastor there. It is that simple, yet profound!

Pastors must realize that you cannot give what you don't have. Pastors will only be able to reproduce who they really are. Yes, people follow Christ, but they will only follow Him to the degree they see Him in Pastors.

The bottomline is that people still have a desire to hear authentic word from God through an authentic servant of God.

Being a Pastor is an awesome responsibility because the people seek for a change and power that is outside of themselves. They come to church with the hope that you will remind them that their lives matter, that God cares, that there is hope and that preparation for life after this life must be made here and now.

Unfortunately, majority of Pastors of today are no longer speaking forthrightly to the people. All the hue and cry about the sad situations of the church and ungodly happenings can be traced directly to the wrong kind of Pastors in control of churches.

Without steadfast, dynamic, godly and informed Pastors, there can be no thriving and vital churches. Society cannot flourish without godly and effective Pastors. The condition of the churches today are simply the replica of the kinds of Pastors leading them.

In my years of training and interaction with many Pastors, I have come to discover various kinds of Pastors and their characteristics. This chapter is an attempt to describe them. I give credit to one of my sons in the Lord for sending me a good write up about this issue and I have to adapt and rework them to fit into this chapter.

While this book is being revised I sincerely hope every Pastor will see this chapter as a mirror that will really reveal the type of Pastor he is. You must identify yourself and change where necessary. True change and growth in the Pastor will lead to same in the church.

> Without steadfast, dynamic, godly and informed Pastors, there can be no thriving and vital churches

Every Sunday, ten of thousands of Pastors mount the pulpit to preach and talk to people. They have different motives for preaching, they have different characters, habits and believe.

While some are happy, others are hungry. While some are dangerous, others are saints. While some are real, others are fake and charlatans.

Now, every Pastor must answer this question in a personal way; what kind of Pastor are you? Discover yourself in these descriptions of various kinds of Pastors:

1. **Businessmen Pastors:**

They are basically business minded men and women who see the ministry as an avenue to make money. They are less concerned about the souls of men.

They build their churches based on business principles and they function as the Chief Executive Officers. Their motive is gain and profit. What matters most is what percentage of money is coming through their various programmes.

Programmes are simply avenues to make more and more money. They will preach the kinds of message that will make people happy and open their wallets.

Their church is a spiritual Business School. Every financial principle is taught in the church. Businessmen Pastors are found in Denominational Churches too. They are expert, in visitation. Of course, such visitations are directed towards the rich members only, the sick and the poor are not included.

These set of Pastors do steal money from the church. If anyone gives some amount of money to the church through them, they will convert it to their own. Their slogan is 'he that work on the altar should eat from the altar!'

They are bunch of liars and crooks. They always lie about their membership, ministration and giving. They don't allow anyone to count the money after each programme, except themselves.

They are not interested in discipling anybody, since they themselves are not discipled. Their strategy of going on air through Television and Radio is not because they really want to preach the gospel of the kingdom, but a business strategy to woo and win

people to support them financially.
Pastor, is this not who you are?

2. **Funky Pastors:**

These are worldly Pastors, leading immoral churches. They want to have the best of the world and the kingdom of God. They allow anything in the church.

You can dress anyhow, live your life the way you please. Girls and women can wear body hug dresses, spaghetti, see-through, mini-skirts and revealing pants, all to the glory of God.

Their assertion is that God looks at the heart, not what you put on. Their wives do dress to kill also. At times they dress and look like Pentecostal Jezebels.

Pastors too come to church with any kind of hair-cut; jerry curls, plaiting the hair and rings, neck-laces and ear rings. In those kinds of places, immorality, carnality, infighting and ungodliness are the order of the day.

Many of such Pastors are on the Television and millions are following them because theirs is a 'church of liberty'; ministry on the broad road; their message is centered around **"easy way to heaven"** , **"prosperity without tears"** etc.

No teaching about sin, holiness and righteousness is allowed and no mention of hell must be made. The focus must be miracle, blessing, prosperity and financial breakthrough.

Youths enjoy these kinds of Pastors, because they have liberty to date, co-habitate, and toast the opposite sex. Holy kiss is allowed and you don't have to pray to choose a marriage partner again, just 'shine your eyes'.

Immorality and extra-marital affairs are swept under the carpet in churches being lead by funky Pastors. Serious Bible truths are explained away and people are told to just worship the Lord, and everything will be okay.

Pastor, does this description not fit you?

3. **Vocational Pastors:**

These set of Pastors are largely in the ministry, not as a result of the call of God, but as a result of the call of men. They have their jobs and also take up this work as a hobby or a past-time. They love the prestige, honour and respect being given to Pastors and therefore decide to share in it.

They became Pastors as a result of tribal sentiments, ethnic bias, connection to the highest authority, wealth, status and oratory power. They used educational qualifications, charisma, showmanship and greasing of palms with assorted gifts to attain the position of Pastors.

Sometimes, they are labelled as honorary Pastors, who are there just to lord over the people. Since they don't have a genuine call from the Lord, they usually don't have any vision to share and pursue. Their churches are always monotonous, stereotyped, powerless and lifeless.

Vocational Pastors always demand for respect, obedience and submission from members. They are full of themselves and do not relate with anyone. Their loyalty is to the person that appointed and ordained them.

In very many cases, Vocational Pastors love to rule and dominate full time and God-called Pastors. They always bring secular management system to bear on the day-to-day running of the church. They enact policies that always lead the church backward.

Since they are too busy with their daily jobs, they have no time to attend to the spiritual needs of the people. Their ministration is largely devoid of God's power and their words are ordinary letters that lack the power of the Spirit.

The spiritual condition of a church always goes from bad to worse when a Vocational Pastor is in control. People's lives will be shallow, carnal, ungodly and caricature of true Christians. Despite all these glaring effects, Vocational Pastors don't really care, so long their prestige and respect is intact.

Are you one of such Pastors?

4. **Yesterday's Pastors:**

These are Pastors of Denominational churches. In some instances, they are found among some independent but old churches. They are largely uneducated and have very poor dress sense.

> Yesterday's Pastors have very low relational skills, the more reason they don't delegate and work through people

They are being driven by the past moves of God. They are ultra-conservatives in their views and are prejudiced against growth, change and new strategies.

Though they are holy, godly and righteous, yet they are not in tune with the moves of God for today. The can pray but they are lacking in real Bible knowledge.

They are contented with old tradition, church dogma and doctrinal correctness. They have no vision of changing the world. They are good in hymnals, bell-ringing and order of service that have lost meaning and purpose.

Yesterday's Pastors have very low relational skills, the more reason they don't delegate and work through people. They do everything alone in the church and will not train anyone to do the work along with them. They always view change with alarm and their desire is to bring back the old time religion.

Pastors of yesterday are always confused with the situation of things in the church today. They have been left behind in the changes that have taken place in the world.

Because they are backward in their views, their churches also are backward and are unable to win the people of today. Pastors of yesterday run church like the days of our great grand fathers, the more reason there is so much stagnation, breakaway, crisis and backdoor loses. Pastors of yesterday usually don't know the new moves of God for today, they are too busy looking at yesterday.

Pastor, are you one of them or are you still current?

5. **Political Pastors:**

These are Pastors that were once servants of the Lord, but due to economic hardship, influence of bad friends and acceptance of strange teachings, have now become servants of the people. Their faithfulness is no longer to the Lord, but now to the people. They are available to the highest bidder. They do things to satisfy the people.

If a wealthy member commits fornication, they will stop preaching about immorality so as not to offend him. They are democratic Pastors. They are in the habit of following and carrying out the decision of the Boards, Committee and financial backers of the church.

They are political leaders who love and spend good time playing church politics. They are cunning, crafty, arm-twisting and can speak from both sides of the mouth. They are equally engrossed in denominational politics of transfer, discipline, suspension and outright sack of fellow Pastors.

They are very close to leaders in their denomination and know how to play their cards so that they are strategically placed in positions of power and authority in their churches. They always move from one meeting to the other, until they have no time to pray, read and study the Bible for personal edification again.

Of course, their churches always suffer, because they are not always around due to frequent meetings. The frequency of such meetings usually leave them spiritually dry until they get involved in scandals and there will be lots of maneuvering to cover up.

These kinds of Pastors are largely found in Denominational churches and some old independent churches.

Are you one of them?

> Pastors of yesterday usually don't know the new moves of God for today, they are too busy looking at yesterday

6. Occultic Pastors:

These are Pastors that have no business being in the ministry, but they are there all the same. They live double lives. They are saints and righteous in the church, but they are sinners and dirty in their hearts and in private. They pretend to eat at the table of the Lord, but also dine with the devil. They use means and demonic power to perform spurious miracles.

They are found among Spiritual, Charismatic and Pentecostal churches. Some of them do have concubines, marry two or more wives, divorce and remarry at will, sleep with their Secretaries and Choir members in the name of prophetic ministration and deliverance sessions. They use candles, coconut, incense, salt, kolanut, sponge, soaps and native roots as "prayer support". They engage in fake vision, false prophecy and "thus says the Lord" that only comes from the pit of hell.

In a nutshell, majority of these Pastors are herbalists, pure and simple! But they hoodwink people by their spurious and spooky miracles. They profess to go to sixth or seventh heaven to procure miracle for people. Most of those people that claim miraculous solution to their problems in most of their meetings always relapse back to their problems.

Occultic Pastors believe that they are helping God and the people to solve their problems. Though they try to do it with oath of secrecy, yet God always reveal their secrets. Of course, people under such devilish Pastors will be in bondage and nightmares will be common. There can be no form of godly spirituality in such places.

Are you relying only on the name, blood and word of Jesus or have you added another thing?

7. **Shallow Pastors:**

These type of Pastors are proud, garrulous and have a very high view of themselves. They are an island, because they are always too big or busy to read anybody's book, listen to anybody's tape and attend ministers conferences and seminars that have the power to refresh and renew them.

They believe everyone should learn from them, but they cannot learn from anybody. If they happen to find themselves under any ministration, they find it hard to open their Bibles and take down notes.

Their 'anointing' has grown to the extent that they don't need to read the Bible everyday, have quiet time or fast.

They now give talk about their wardrobe, shoes, cars and achievements in place of the true and undiluted word of God. Their messages are now dry, no more mystery but stories.

Though, they give the appearance of being full and loaded, yet the truth is that these men are dry, shallow and empty barrels that make lots of noise. They try to cover their dryness and shallowness with stage demonstration, shouting, anointing oil and carnal performances of pushing people down under the guise of anointing and deliverance.

Of course, serious members will know that something is wrong and many will move away to feed themselves where the grass is still green.

Pastor, how do you fare in this regard?

8. **Ministry Pastors:**

These are ministry focused Pastors. They are committed and consumed by the work of the ministry. They are busy working for the Lord but have almost lost the Lord of the work. They will neglect their families, children and personal lives in the name of the ministry. Their children are therefore wayward, bitter, uncatered for, angry and unconverted. Their wives are miserable, frustrated, neglected, feel cheated and lonely.

> Ministry Pastors are busy working for the Lord but have almost lost the Lord of the work

These Pastors usually move from meetings to meetings, crusades to revivals, from prayer mountains to prayer retreats.

When they are around, which is not often, they visit, counsel members, prepare their Sunday sermons and attend committee meetings until late in the night.

They don't have time to relax, play and enjoy with their wives, children and family members. They are always in a hurry and must attend to one church matter or the other. They are too holy to play, talk, plan and share with their spouses.

Of course such Pastors have missed it. They usually experience divorce, wayward children and unfulfilled ministry. The church will eventually reject them because of the bad examples of their families.
Ministry Pastors also have wives that become demonised and engage in extra-marital affairs due to lack of care and attention.

Pastors that give ministry the number one priority above their God, home and personal development will always experience crisis, breakaway and being forsaken by the Lord. Lack of peace, progress and tranquility, both in the church and personal lives will always be the outcome of the mistake of putting ministry before God and your family.

Pastor, are you really free from this type of pastoral life?

9. **Sick Pastors:**

In most cases, these set of Pastors are physically okay but are spiritually sick. They are sick because they are not free from sin, evil, immorality and wickedness. Though they sometimes lead large congregations, but their spiritual sickness soon catch up with them and the church nose-dive. They have backslided from following the Lord. They now use spiritual activities to cover their spiritual nakedness.

Sick Pastors are carnal, ungodly and worldly-minded Pastors. They have lost their vision, plan and purpose of being in the ministry. They were once on fire for the Lord, but have now lost it due to walking at the brink of sin.

Such Pastors lack basic leadership skills. They speak anyhow to anybody, do anything, eat anywhere, get angry, even on the pulpit, take rash decisions, hurl insults and abuse their perceived enemies.

Sick Pastors are impatient, openly castigate their wives in the church, and they display so much stinginess, covetousness, unforgiving spirit and unreliable in anything.

They pick quarrel with members easily, pray dangerous prayers, pull down potential leaders and are ready to do anything to destroy whoever strays across their path.

Sick Pastors are cursed Pastors. They started the ministry on wrong foundation of lying, deceit and offending their senior Pastors. Though, their churches might experience a high turn over of members,

> Pastors that give ministry the number one priority above their God, home and personal development will always experience crisis, breakaway and being forsaken by the Lord

yet the wrong foundation always work against them.

People are wearied and frustrated at the actions of such Pastors. Their churches will never know peace because the Pastors themselves are troublesome. They actually created the situation whereby fighting and quarreling will erupt.

Incidentally, such Pastors don't see themselves as the problem of the church. Rather, they point accusing fingers at members, workers and associates.

Sick Pastors will always produce sick churches that will find growth very difficult.

Are you a sick or a healthy Pastor?

10. Wounded Pastors:

These kinds of Pastors came into the ministry with high hopes but they soon found out that ministry is hard. Through some mistakes and carelessness, these men and women of God have been wounded in the battle.

They were wounded by sin, devil, people and partners. Ministry has dealt them a hard blow. Sometimes, they lose their children, wives, husbands, families and wealth because of ministry.

Furthermore, many have been wounded by associates, supporters, leaders and mentors. And the wound is fresh and new. These acts of betrayal in the ministry has left many Pastors' hearts bleeding and bitter. They are therefore discouraged, despondent, frustrated and tired. As a result, some have packed up their ministries while some are at the verge of quitting.

Many Pastors that are walking wounded today are nursing one form of wound or the other in their hearts. They are trying hard to forgive the betrayal, backstabbing and injustice meted out to them by supposed friends and Christians. The breakaway, church crisis, mud-sligging upon their name came as an outcome of these betrayals.

> Many have been wounded by associates, supporters, leaders and mentors and the wound is fresh and new

Such Pastors therefore find it hard to trust people. They have decided not to train or help anybody in the ministry again and take any offer of help with a pinch of salt. They become skeptical of others' intentions because their wound is still fresh and sore.

Of course, God's Spirit will no longer flow in great ways through such Pastors because they have refused to forgive the past and march on. Their ministry will never be able to fulfil its potential as long as those hurts are in the heart.

As long as you don't allow the Lord to heal you, your church will always suffer the hangover of your wounded heart.

Pastor, what kind of wound are you battling with?

11. Technology Pastors:

These are the Pastors on the move, Pastors on the fast lane of life. They move from city to city, nation to nation making money at the expense of the soul of those under their care. In some cases, they spend three weeks away in a month and come back for one week, only to go abroad again.

As the Pastor travels from Continent to Continent, he continues to monitor the church through phone, e-mails, websites and phone-in-conference. He uses these technology to conduct services, prays over the telephone set connected to the public address system at vigils and Sunday services.

In other instances, the Pastors stay abroad permanently, yet they preach and control the church through these technologies. The question is what are they doing over there? They are making money and enjoying themselves!

At other times, the church only listens to audio tapes of the messages of the Pastor every week so that they can keep following Him. The associates are not trusted and relied upon to do a good job, even after they have been properly trained.

Many of such Pastors lose God in the course of much traveling. They usually fall flat on their faces before the god of money, pleasure and evil of this world, and are abandoned by God. But they will be covering up with past glories of who they were before.

Many of them eventually lose their churches and

ministries. God always do away with them and replace them with capable people who will do a better job.

12. **Growing Pastors:**

Though very few, yet these are Pastors after God's heart. They are called and commissioned by the Lord. They maintain their relationship with the Lord despite the pressure of work and ministry.

They don't only read the Bible to preach, but for personal edification. They fight and strive to maintain their prayer lives, and they never compromise with sin and evil deeds. They are not perfect, but they are growing in the things of the Lord. They are hot for the Lord and they desire and work to make serious impact upon their world.

These Pastors build great integrity, transparency, character and trustworthiness into their daily and ministerial lives. They combine spiritual gifts with the fruit of the Spirit. They are fruitful and careful. They are in tune with the Spirit and are open to change and the leading of God on any issue.

Growing Pastors see the ministry as opportunity to serve others. They de-emphasis money, profit and gain. Their heart desire is to please the Lord and build His kingdom, not their personal empire.

They build the church on His undiluted word. They are clear about the standard of holiness, godliness and distinct lifestyles that is required of every genuine Christian.

A growing Pastor is a disciple of Jesus and therefore embarks on discipling the Christians in his church. They don't believe in the Christianity that cost you nothing. They outline the cost of being disciples and demand obedience to them.

Of course, they lead growing, dynamic, effective and lively churches for the Lord. People experience transformation, turn-around and God's favour in the church because the Pastors are connected to God.

> Growing Pastors see the ministry as opportunity to serve others. Their heart desire is to please the Lord and build His kingdom, not their personal empire

In a church being pastored by a growing Pastor, the people will discover and utilize their gifts without let or hindrance. They use their gifts to bring growth to the church. The Pastor encourages their giftings and ministries. He is not worried by inferiority complex, neither is he threatened by their gift and calling. He will raise up leaders and equip them to carry on the work of God. A growing Pastor is a learner. He continually invest in himself so that he can keep abreast of change in the ministry.

From these description of twelve kinds of Pastors, you can see that only one can really lead the church to growth. This is the reason why majority of churches are sick, stagnant and dying today because they are being pastored by the wrong kind of Pastors. Denominational leaders will do well to take note of these kinds of Pastors.

    Moreover, Pastors that find themselves in any of the first eleven can repent and change today and now. It's not too late to change and become a growing Pastor that God will use to bring growth to His church.

Healthy Pastoral Leadership | 6

> "Poor growth is the result of poor leadership. Good growth is the result of good leadership. Great growth is the outcome of great and outstanding leadership" - *Francis Bola Akin - John.*

I am not the first person, neither will I be the last to write on leadership. Much have been written, taught and expounded on it, yet not much have changed in terms of true and lasting leadership.

I have spent the last couple of years teaching Church Growth, Vision, Leadership, and sundry subjects to quite a sizable number of Pastors and Church Leaders.

During those times, I have been able to analysed, researched, evaluated and studied so many churches, Pastors and general church leadership styles. My conclusion is that there is much to be desired in terms of healthy leadership in the church. There is crisis of leadership everywhere.

In this chapter, I will focus mainly on pastoral leadership. The Pastor is the number one leader in the local church. The type of leadership he provides will go a long way to determine the growth of the church.

From the beginning of this book, I have been mentioning pastoral leadership here and there. But I am dwelling much on it here because I firmly believe it is the key to the whole essence of church growth.

WHO LEADS THE LOCAL CHURCH?

Many General Overseers, Church Founders and Denominational Heads today have unwittingly surrendered leadership to lower forces. They have placed Boards, Trustees and Executive Committees over and above the Pastors and leaders in the order of things.

This singular act has done much havoc to the church in Nigeria more than any other factor. Many church crisis, breakaways and "guilf war" between Pastors and Church Elders or Board grew out of this man-made error.

Many churches who found themselves in law courts can trace their problem to this issue. Many Patriachs and Matriachs or pioneers in the church have taken it as a normal pastime to oppose and resist the

Pastor once he is not doing things their own way! The root of many stagnant, crisis-ridden, prostrate and non-growing churches are attributable to this lingering problem. What then shall we do? How do we go about solving this problem?

> Many Pastors who found themselves in leadership positions in the church are largely ignorant of what healthy leadership is all about

Well, I strongly recommend that the Pastor must be the leader in the church and the Boards, Committee, Trustee or whichever name you prefer should support the Pastor. They are to act as check and balances. The only time they can take control is when the Pastor delegates, not around, or has resigned or withdrawn due to moral or financial failure.

This position is supported by the Scriptures and experience. In Revelation Chapters 2 and 3, God sent messages to the angel, not angels or committee of the church. He recognized the angel - in this case the Pastor, in-charge of each local assembly. The Pastor is the set man, the eye, hand and representative of God in the local assembly. He must be honoured and respected.

Deacons, Elders and Committee that unnecessarily oppose and antagonize Pastors are courting God's wrath. The church is the only property of God on earth and He will always deal with those who cause chaos and crisis. When you carelessly touch God's authority, God's authority will touch you also.

In the wilderness, God communed and communicated only with Moses and he inturn relayed it back to the children of Israel (Ps. 103:7). At no time did God communed or showed His ways to a Committee, but to one man. He will always talk to the man in control because God respects and honours leadership.

It's time we start to appreciate Pastors among and around us. The peace and progress of our churches lies in abiding by this principle of the Lord.

One more thing I like to add is that Pastors must be properly and well remunerated. Across the board, I am aware that Pastors are poorly paid and many are finding it difficult to feed. This is too bad. Churches that suffer Pastors are placing themselves under perpetual curse that will be difficult to break.

WHAT IS HEALTHY PASTORAL LEADERSHIP?

When the Pastor has been duly recognized as the main leader in the church and treated as such, he is duty bound to provide healthy leadership if the church is to grow.

Unfortunately, I have to admit that many Pastors who found themselves in leadership positions in the church are largely ignorant of what healthy leadership is all about. They are sadly unaware that nothing is as important to the growth of the church as the kind of leadership being provided. They have forgotten the words of John Maxwell: "Everything rises and falls on leadership".

Many have wrongly thought that leadership is anointing, gifts, talents, age, education and status. No, one may have all of the above without necessarily being a leader.

Healthy leadership is very complex. It has many facet such as: vision, character, experience, emotional strength, skills, relationship, etc. You may dress, talk, walk and live like a leader and have titles that suggest that you are a leader. However, if you don't possess a God-given call and vision to your people, you are not a leader.

The church is the most leadership intensive organization in the whole world and if the Pastor is not providing the healthy leadership that the people could identify with, the church will not grow nor be healthy.

Before I go on to give the essential qualities of healthy pastoral leadership, allow me to compare and contrast sick and healthy leadership:

Sick Leadership	**Healthy leadership:**
* Fight, tussle and connection to gain position.	* Called by the Lord
* Proud and garrulous of title and position.	* Humble and self-effacing

* Words does not march action	*Marches words with appropriate action.
* Drives his workers and people.	* Coaches his workers and trains his people.
* Depends on authority and power.	* Depends on goodwill and influence.
* Inspires fear and dread	* Inspires enthusiasm.
* Says "I"	* Says "We"
* Threatened by gifts and abilities of others	* Happy to see leaders developed.
* Fixes blame for breakdown	* Fixes the breakdown.
* Knows only how it is done	* Shows how it is done.
* Doesn't tolerate question or explanation.	*Explains reason for actions.
* Says "go"	* Says "let's go"
* Manipulative and abusive	* Motivates and inspires
* No room for personal growth	*Creates room for personal fulfillment.
* Uses people to grow a great church.	* Uses church to grow a great people.
* De-emphasise people's importance	*Stresses peoples importance.

* Critical and unappreciative of efforts.	* Create room to thank and appreciate the support of His people.

The above table shows the great difference between sick and healthy leadership. The more you tend towards the healthy side, the better your church. But the more you move towards the left side, the worse would be your church.

One good thing about leadership is that you can improve on it. Leadership skills can be learned. Leadership is an art that can be developed over a period of time. The greatest test of leadership is not where you started, but where you ended.

You can become a better leader today by constantly working at improving your leadership skills. Leadership doesn't develop in a day. It takes a life-time. Some Pastors who are administrators and managers don't usually see much growth. Great growth can only come when the Pastor concentrates on being a true leader.

EFFECTIVE PASTORAL LEADERSHIP

Pastors in local churches can provide healthy leadership that will culminate in growth, increase, expansion, turnaround and health of their churches if they will learn and practise the following principles.

The cry all over the world is for effective pastors. And you can become one when you follow these:

1. **Vision:**

Leadership have been described as the capacity to rally people behind a common objective. In other words, it is the capacity to lead people towards the realization of a vision. Leadership therefore has much to do with capacity to translate vision into reality. No vision, nothing to lead for.

> Vision of who we are, where we are going and how we are going to get there must be constantly placed before the people

One indispensable trait of healthy leadership is vision. Healthy leadership is sensing and obeying God's call to fulfil a particular vision and empowering your people along the line.

In the Scriptures, everyone that God called was given a vision to accomplish. Noah was to build the ark; Abraham was to become the head of a new race of people; Joseph was to preserve people in famine; Moses was to lead the people to freedom; Joshua was to divide the promised land to them and so on and so forth.

Those who have powerfully and permanently influenced our world today are men of vision.

Everything we enjoy in life today are the outcome of someone's vision. To truly lead effectively there must be vision. For the people to truly rise up and rally round the Pastor, he must communicate God's vision for the church in a clear and understandable way.

Vision of who we are, where we are going and how we are going to get there must be constantly placed before the people. People will not rise to a battle cry they have never heard. People commit themselves more to a vision than to a personality.

Vision brings unity, commitment, victory, focus, planning, evaluation, strategy and momentum in the church. When you are out of vision you are out of leadership. If you are not appointed, you will be disappointed. If He has not commanded you, He will not be committed to you.

2. **Influence:**

Effective pastoral leadership in the church demands that more than anybody else, the Pastor must possess the ability to influence. Most teachings and study about leadership have largely neglected the basic importance of influence, yet we cannot do without it.

Leadership is leadership no matter where you go or what you do. Time changes, technology marches on. Culture varies from place to place but the true principles of leadership are constant.

Most importantly, the church is the most

leadership intensive enterprise in the world. This is so because positional leadership doesn't work much if a leader doesn't have influence. In other organizations, if all else fails, the leader can rely on his position to cow the people into submission, but in the church, leaders only have their influence to aid them.

Power of Influence: - Most Pastors have sadly not understood the power of influence. The Elders, Deacons, Boards and Committee members know more about the power of influence than most Pastors.

People in these category of leadership have devised and perfected means of gaining influence in the church. They will use strategic positioning, money, authority, goodwill, care, giving, character assassinations, church tradition, and sometimes commitment, gifts, talents and loving relationship with members to gain more influence. Many times these influences can work positively or negatively against the church.

It is high time that Pastors understand clearly that leadership is influence - no more, no less! What is influence? Influence simply means ability to make people follow you without you forcing them.

No one can truly understand that mysterious thing called influence, yet everyone of us continually

> Influence simply means ability to make people follow you without you forcing them

exerts influence, either to heal, bless, beautify or to wound, hurt or to poison and to stain others' lives. The Pastor influences, the parents influence their children and the teachers influence their pupils. Music, books, words, characters, manners, dressing and examples, all influence positively or negatively.

Influence cannot be managed, it must be earned. Influence doesn't come automatically, it comes in stages. Without influence people will not follow you and if people don't follow you, you are not a leader.

Real healthy leadership is being the person others will gladly and confidently follow. And the Pastor must epitomes such. There can be no success, followership, attainment and impact if the Pastor is not the most influential person in the church.

To be the most influential person in the church, it will take the Pastor at least two to three years. It takes time before you can influence people. Your relationship with people, your integrity, godly character, results and reproduction in ministry and ultimately, your person and personality will greatly enhance the level of your influence. The more you work on these areas the more you will be able to lead people and greater will be the growth of the church.

When your people see in you a true model and they discover you are ready to nurture, motivate, mentor and multiply them, they will surrender themselves to be influenced by you and greater will be the growth of the work. When you have come to the place that strong trust and bond exist between you and your people, then you can influence them positively for kingdom growth.

3. People Skills

Church growth and leadership requires people-oriented skills. In so many leadership teachings, the place and importance of people is sadly overlooked and hardly given the attention it requires, the more reason for the myriads of problems on our hands.

The greatest asset of leadership is not physical, material, financial and numerical assets, but people. People are the most important asset of leadership. No matter who you are, you cannot get far without the ability to deal with people. Every worthwhile vision will always need the help of others to support and back it up. We will always need the help of others to carry out our vision. How to relate with people, how to motivate people and how to lead people must be mastered by Pastors who want to achieve something worthwhile.

> No matter who you are, you cannot get far without the ability to deal with people. Every worthwhile vision will always need the help of others to support and back it up

People's skills is the sum total of leadership. Pastors must especially be adept in dealing with various editions of men. "The most single ingredient to the formula of success is knowing how to get along with various kinds of people". - Roosevelt.

Types of people in the church - I Thess. 5:14.

1. **The unruly** - stubborn and disobedient people
2. **The feebleminded** - sensitive and critical people
3. **The weak** - Spiritually, physically and psychologically
4. **The strong** - Spiritually, materially and educationally.

Rules and regulations without relationship equals to resentment and rebellion (R+R-R = R+R). On the other hand, rules and regulations combined with relationship equals result and respect (R+R+R = R+R).

We will always have people such as Lot, Korah, Dathan, Abiram, Aaron, Gehazi, Absalom, Judas, Demas and Diotrephes in the church. They were there then, they are there today and they will always be there.

On the other hand we also will not lack people such as Enoch, Abraham, Isaac, Jacob, Joseph, Joshua, Caleb, Samuel, David, Jeremiah, Daniel, Peter, Paul, Timothy and Epaphras. There are so many of them around if you have eyes to see. A leader without people is a crippled man.

People and Leadership:

1. People "buy into" the leader before they "buy into" his vision.
2. People follow someone who is better and stronger than they are.
3. People do not care how much you know until they know how much you care.
4. People need personal attention and approach
5. People need motivation, encouragement, integrity and communication.
6. People are skeptical of both secular and spiritual leaders as a result of much disappointments.
7. People don't expect perfection from leaders, but desires humility, integrity and openness.

If you raise men, you will never be erased from the earth. Dealing with people requires wisdom, maturity, patience, love, endurance, forgiving spirit, tenderness, toughness, boldness, humility and perseverance.

Many leaders and churches have lost key people that could have made a difference and continue to loose such people due to the following points. These points will pinpoint what puts people off from church leaders:

1. Insensitivity
2. Belittleness

3. Sinfulness and hypocrisy
4. No room for personal development
5. Rigidity and narrow-mindedness
6. Unforgiving spirit
7. Impervious to suggestion and advises
8. Lack of care and opportunities
9. Generosity with criticism and miserly with praise
10. Inability to admit mistakes and apologize.

Likewise, people demand the following from every church leader:

1. Believe in people
2. Encourage them
3. Share with them
4. Trust in them
5. Train them
6. Invest in them
7. Give them a chance
8. Help them to keep going.

> Every time you take a problem, confront and succeed in solving it, then followers will have another reason to trust your leadership

4. Solving Problems and Initiating Change:

True leaders must solve problems. It is not enough to set the vision, exert influence and relate well with people, there must also be the ability to solve problems.

Multifarious problems will confront the church.

They will come in various ways and through various means. The Pastor - leader must possess the capacity to deal with those problems squarely without losing his perspectives.

Nothing speaks to followers like a good track record. Every time you take a problem, confront and succeed in solving it, then followers will have another reason to trust your leadership and listen to what you have to say. Part of the problem the Pastor-leader must confront head long is change. The leader must function as an agent of change.

The leader as an agent of change is either representing the change or the person who wants change. Many leaders prefer to be agents of tradition in the church because they don't want to ruffle some feathers. But effective pastoral leadership that will lead the church of the new millennium must be agents of change.

God is looking for leaders that are change agents. Change can be positive as in creating or regenerating it and can also be negative as in rebellion or overthrow. Positive change is creating a better future than returning to a cherished past of chaos and crisis.

Three truths for leaders who are agents of change:

1. You have been changed in the past
2. You must be willing to change today and

3. You must face the problems of leading people through change.

"You cannot grow if you don't change. Change is growth. Not every change is progress, but we cannot progress if we don't change". A leader's success in bringing about change in others and the church will happen only if the timing is right.

Why do people resist change?

1. The change isn't self-initiated.
2. Routine is disrupted.
3. Contentment with the way things are
4. Fear of the unknown
5. Purpose of change is not clear
6. Fear of failure and lowering of 'standards'
7. Negative thinking
8. Lack of respect for the leader
9. Narrow-mindedness
10. Clinging to tradition
11. Fear of personal loss.

Those closest to the leader feels the change much more than others. The more reason we must communicate clearly. Imperfect leaders, imperfect people, imperfect communication, imperfect understanding and imperfect relationship all lead to barrier to change and innovations.
-   Wrong decision at the wrong time equals

- disaster
- Wrong decision at the right time equals mistake
- The right decision at the wrong time equals unacceptance
- The right decision at the right time equals success!

To initiate change in the church, the leader must develop trust with the people. Trust is the emotional glue that binds leaders and followers together.

The leader must also make personal change before others will change. The more you change, the more you become an instrument of change to others. If you want to become a change agent, you must also change. If you want to continue leading, you must continue changing.

Finally, I sincerely hope that those in position of pastoral leadership will take these qualities very seriously and continue to work on them if they hope to become very effective in leading the people of God to greater heights.

I am devoting the next chapter to one more salient factor that has and will continue to influence church leadership more than any other factors.

Pastor's Personal Growth 7

"Your personal growth is the growth of your work"
- *Francis Bola Akin-John.*

Growth is the fact of life, the purpose of our existence. We live to grow and grow to live. Nowhere is this one true than in the life of the minister. No ministry has grown enough.

Ministerial and ministry growth are like siamese twins, there can be no one without the other. Attempt to separate the two will always lead to death.

In the effort to bring growth, increase and expansion to the church, we have laid so much emphasis on methods, machinery and money. We have tried to reduce the place and importance of the man. Yet we need to understand that God is more infinitely concerned with the man that heads the church than anything else.

Much of the blame for lack of growth in the church are laid squarely at the foot of the members. The Pastors are usually omitted and for that reason alone will want to exonerate himself regarding the conditions of the church.

True, in some situations, the people are responsible, but in most cases the problem rests with the Pastors more. In reality, 60% of the growth problems in the church will start with the Pastor. It is an unwritten law that the church will become what the minister is.

Our ministry, International Church Growth Ministries has viewed with alarm the myriad of problems brought upon the church by the lack of growth of the Pastor. We have been alarmed at the high rate of ministerial casualties, disgrace and dishonour brought upon the church. And we know that if the personal growth of the minister is taken seriously, most of these disgracing episodes will be greatly minimised.

Personal growth is the primary growth. It is the greatest price of leadership. The leadership that refuses to pay the price of personal growth will soon forfeit it. This price of leadership in the church cannot be paid in a lump sum, once or forever. No! It must be paid installmentally and gradually.

It is quite revealing that many Pastors are unaware of this fact. They behave, live, talk and minister as if they don't need to grow anymore. The day your personal growth stops, that day your leadership stops. This price is too much for many leaders to pay, the more reason they are losing their leadership.

Personal growth or lack of it will show in every area of your life. Your leadership, home, relationships, ministry and future will be helped or hindered by your personal growth.

DEFINING PERSONAL GROWTH

Personal growth could be described from various angles. It means growing in relationship with the Lord; more maturity of heart and life; attaining great heights spiritually (Phi. 3:10-14); moving from grave to grass, from grass to grace, from grace to glory, and from glory to glory.

It means building your character, greater integrity and godliness. Adding more to your faith as Apostle Peter says in II Peter 1:5-10. It also comes in form of attitudinal changes, having a broad shoulder and a large heart to accommodate people and

> Your growth determines who you are, who you are determines who you attract and who you attract determines the success of your ministry

various kinds of views. It could also come in the area of overcoming a particular weakness and breaking of bad habits in your life. It shows in positive changes and more patience and maturity in handling issues of life.

Personal growth covers five major areas:

*   **Spiritual maturity** - Your spiritual stature determines much.
*   **Emotional maturity** - Self-control, self-mastering.
*   **Mental maturity** - Information, learning, wisdom and knowledge.
*   **Social maturity** - Relating effectively with people.
*   **Communication maturity** - Ability to motivate and draw out the best in people.

Technologies, systems and ideas may change; 'hot leadership' secrets and big breaks may come, but the place of personal growth never changes.

I sincerely consider the pastoral job as the toughest job in the whole world. Pastors are operating under intense pressures. The demands are sometimes too high and many Pastors are quitting the ministry due to moral failure, frustration and lack of resources.

Nowhere is personal growth more paramount than in the pastoral ministry. The Pastor deals with various types of people. Sometimes people who are more educated, more exposed, much older, quite younger and more richer than him are all under his pastorate. He definitely needs divine wisdom to minister effectively and lead them, week in, week out.

Effective and lasting leadership demands constant availability to growth and transformation in the above mentioned five areas. Your growth determines who you are, who you are determines who you attract and who you attract determines the success of your ministry.

POWER OF PERSONAL GROWTH

Growth does not start outside of you but begins inside of you. The growth of your church is determined by your inner growth. Your inner growth will go a long way to determine your outward growth. You must be bigger within before you can be bigger without. If you don't be, you cannot do. This is what Jesus made Nicodemus to understand. He came to Jesus seeing only what He is doing. But Jesus made him to see that being is more important than doing.

Until we are what we should be, we cannot do what we should do. (John 3:1-3). It goes without saying then, that the speed of the leader is the speed of the organization. Grow the Pastor, grow the church, grow the leader, grow the organization.

The ability to lead rises and falls with the personal growth of the leader. When your growth stops, your ability to lead stops with it.

The leader that hopes to lead his church to great heights must always start with his own personal development. God is much interested with the personal growth of the minister. He uses various means to accomplish this.

In the truest sense of the word, many of the problems, oppositions, trials, precautions, misrepresentations and crisis in our lives were designed by God to aid our personal growth and prepare us for better leadership. If God loves you dearly, He will hurt you deeply.

> The leader that hopes to lead his church to great heights must always start with his own personal development

The fact that God is using you doesn't mean you should stop growing. The devil has used these activities to deceive many that they don't need to grow anymore. They failed to take notice of the slips, sins, faults and weaknesses in their lives because they are being mightily used by God. Sadly, many have found out too late that personal growth must never stop despite His usage.

Personal growth is the:

* **Key to ministry growth** - Your ministry will never rise higher than your growth.
* **Key to growing others** - You cannot demand from others what you don't demand from yourself
* **Key to finishing well** - To finish strong and not die along the way demand for constant growth.
* **Key to outstanding leadership** - Your leadership level or ability is greatly determined by your growth.
* **Key to higher calling** - To move to higher degree of ministry success will be helped or hindered by your personal growth.
* **Key to handling success successfully** - Many have been ruined by their seeming success because of lack of personal growth.
* **Key to overcoming the storms of life** - Personal growth will enable you to sail through the storms of life that will inevitably come across your way.

TEN DON'TS OF PERSONAL GROWTH

Do not surrender means don't give up, stop or quit on the ground of one challenge or the other. Therefore these are things you must never surrender your personal growth to:

1. Don't surrender your personal growth to **Circumstances**

Your circumstances and condition may be pathetic, no helper or supporter. There may be practically no way or means of embarking on the journey of personal development. Yet you must not give up. Remember, your condition does not matter but what matters is your conclusion. Remember Gideon. The conditions were terrible but he found a way to grow.

> You cannot do what you should do, until you are what you should be

2. Don't surrender your personal growth to **Success:**

Success has destroyed much more people than failure. If you allow your success so far to handle you, it will ruin you. Rather, grow to the level whereby you can handle your success very successfully. Remember Judas. His little success got into his head and it ruined him. Don't let past success hinder your better future. There is no future in the past and there is no past in the future.

3.   Don't surrender your personal growth to **Anointing**

Today, the popular jargon is anointing. Many are seeking anointing despite lack of good character foundation. Without godly character, the anointing alone ruins. Many who relied on the anointing without strong character have gotten themselves to blame like Samson. The perennial problems of gold, glory and girls call for serious personal growth.

4.   Don't surrender your personal growth to **Achievement:**

Your personal and ministry achievement will collapse in the absence of personal growth. David achieved much, but his lack of personal growth in his emotions almost ruined his good achievement. Many who rely only on their achievements without corresponding personal development always regret later.

5.   Don't surrender your personal growth to **Methodology**

All the methods in the whole world will fail in the absence of personal growth. You cannot do what you should do, until you are what you should be. Methods, systems, and tactics will change but personal growth remains constant.

6. Don't surrender your personal growth to **Personality:**

Many rely on their natural strong personality to lead people and the church of God. Others rely on their natural abilities. Yet, your strong personality will not suffice without personal growth. You must grow and be tender in God's hand so that He can change you to who He wants you to be. If He leaves you to yourself, you will ruin and destroy not only yourself but the work.

7. Don't surrender your personal growth to **Commendation**

The fact that people are praising and commending you should never make you to abandon personal growth. Noah was praised by God for his godliness and he allowed the commendation to get into his head. When people were committing sin, Noah did not sin, but when people stopped committing sin, Noah started to sin (Gen. 6:8; 9:20-21). You must grow to the level whereby you are able to handle admiration.

8. Don't surrender your personal growth to **Position and Title:**

Positions and titles are loved by many. In actual fact, many are offended when you fail to mention and address them by all the positions and titles they have acquired. Realistically, positions and titles are added burdens and responsibilities.

Quite unfortunately, many are measuring their spiritual stature by their positions and titles. They have been blindfolded from growing personally. Today the craze is for the title of Bishops and Apostles. Formerly it was Reverend Doctor. As much as I have nothing against any prefix or title, my contention is that you must justify such title by the fruit of your labour and don't allow it to hinder your personal growth.

> There are situations that experience and age cannot handle. It is your personal growth that will see you through, coupled with the grace of God

9. Don't surrender your personal growth to **Age and Experience:**

Growth is not a programme, it is a process. Personal growth is a never ending journey. Age and experience cannot replace the role of personal growth. Many are banking on their experience and age to see them through in the ministry. No!

There are situations that will make a mincemeat of whatever is your age or experience. There are situations that experience and age cannot handle. It is your personal growth that will see you through, coupled with the grace of God. Many times, experience is yesterday's solution to today's problems.

10. Don't surrender your personal growth to **Gifts / Talents/ Prophecy:**

Many who are wonderfully gifted, talented and have the prophecy of God concerning a great future awaiting them, but lacks personal growth, discipline and godly character have been ruined by these talents and gifts. Talents, gifts and prophecies alone cannot guarantee lasting success in the ministry. Personal growth will provide the foundation and durability that will sustain you when all else fails.

Things that serve as obstacles and hindrances to personal growth are these:

* **Ignorance** - You don't know your need of it
* **Laziness** - You pamper and self-indulge yourself
* **Self-contentment** - You compare yourself with others.
* **Anti-change and anti-growth** - You believe you are okay and don't need to change anywhere anymore.
* **Lack of clear vision** - Nothing to propel you towards growth.
* **Moving with the wrong people** - Allowing your friends to determine your future.
* **Playing today to pay tomorrow** -

Unwillingness to pay the price for self-development.

FACTORS FOR PERSONAL GROWTH

Personal growth will not happen in a vacuum. There are factors that facilitate it. It is not enough to talk and write about personal growth, we must examine and practise the factors that will enhance it in our lives.

a. **Discover and pursue your life's purpose:** (John 17:4)

Personal growth is not possible if you don't search out God's purpose for your life and pursue it vigorously. God has a purpose for everything He is connected with, including you. Search it out by prayer, fasting, studying yourself and God's dealing with you and be irrevocably committed to its realization. The pursuit of personal growth will only be meaningful and rewarding when you discover God's purpose for your life.

> The best watchman in the whole world is the man that watches carefully over himself

b. **Build a regular and consistent prayer life:** (Luke 1:35).

You cannot rise higher than your prayer life will allow. The major difference between men starts from their prayer life. Your perpetual growth is hinged on your prayer life. Fight for it. Nothing will atone for lack of it.

The flesh, Satan, activities, visitors, work and tiredness will always rise up to hinder your life of prayer. But you must overcome them. Even if you don't feel like praying, pray, pray and pray. Build it up gradually and develop consistency over a period of time. Ministering to the Lord must ever come before ministering to the people. Pastors who are serious about their personal and ministry growth must find time for private prayer.

c. **Work at improving yourself everyday:** (I Cor. 9:27).

Don't ever be satisfied with your present level. Take one area of your life one at a time and work at improving it. Don't be in the habit of excusing evil in your life. Your habit might determine your habitat. Master yourself and be in control of your thoughts, emotions, tongue and reactions. Be a sentinel over your life. The best watchman in the whole world is the man that watches carefully over himself.

d.   **Read, study, read and read -** (I Tim. 4:13; II Tim. 4:13).

Everything you will need to know concerning your calling have been put down in a book by someone. In this age we live in, there is no excuse for ignorance and failure.

A minister is known by the books he reads. Read wide, read deep and study again and again for personal edification and ministration. A learner today is a leader tomorrow. If you stop learning, you stop leading.

Read to edify, motivate, inspire and to gather information that will help you to be a very resourceful minister. The sheep will only come to graze in a very green pasture. You cannot give out what you don't have. Gather knowledge and be informed by attending seminars, conferences and Schools of Ministry.

Conferences and seminars are to ministers what Father Jethro was to Moses. They give you new insight, revelation and new beginning for higher dimension in ministry. Be current and informed about your area of ministry. In this age of computer, e-mail and internet, you dare not be left behind.

e.   **Have a Pastor to Pastor you:**

Your personal growth cannot take a full swing until you have a Pastor to pastor you. You must willingly surrender to someone who can monitor, motivate, challenge, mentor, correct, rebuke and chastise you in the ministry. Someone you respect and who respects and values you. He will serve as a covering to you and give his personal time to raise you to higher level of growth, anointing and success in the ministry.

I am aware of Pastors who have chosen somebody they don't easily see or have personal time with as their mentors. Such Pastors simply chose because of the popularity or achievement of the so-called mentors in the ministry. This is rather unwholesome. Your mentor is someone who can take time to see or visit you and pay close attention to your life, home and ministry.

> Personal prayer partners will through their prayer support bring the growth, maturity, stability and progress you otherwise cannot achieve alone into your life and ministry

f. **Seek for your Prayer Partners:** Eph. 6:18.

This is the icing on the cake. Personal prayer partners will through their prayer support bring the growth, maturity, stability and progress you otherwise cannot achieve alone into your life and ministry.

Many Pastors in Nigeria are ignorant of the

untold benefits of having personal prayer partners of intercessors, yet it is very crucial to this issue of personal growth.

Whoever you are in the ministry, you need prayer partners. Your prayers can never be enough, you will always need the prayer support of others. You are like Joshua in the battle field, you need the prayer support of Moses, Aaron and Hur to gain continuous victory.

The prayer partners can do it part-time or full time basis. They are those who believe strongly in your vision and are willing to support you prayerfully. It usually start with you asking the Lord for such people and God will send someone to you who will do such wonderful ministry.

Peter Wagner stated that "the most under-utilized power in the church is intercession for Pastors". Unlimited personal and church growth is possible when people are praying and "lifting up the hands of their prophet"

GOALS OF PERSONAL GROWTH

1. To be so strong that nothing can disturb your peace of mind.
2. To take health, happiness and prosperity to everyone you meet.
3. To be truly free from every vestige of self life.
4. To be well prepared for the higher calling of God

in Christ Jesus.
5. To make all your friends feel that there is something good in them.
6. To look at the sunny side of everything and be positive all the ways.
7. To think only of the best, work for the best and expect the best.
8. To be obedient, teachable and do things that pleases God always.
9. To have perfect understanding of the actions of others.
10. To always give and give, not expecting much in return.
11. To be truly and sincerely happy and enthusiastic about the success of others without any tinge of envy.
12. To forget the mistakes of the past and press on to the greater achievement of the future.
13. To wear a cheerful countenance at all times and give every person you meet a smile.
14. To give so much time to the improvement of yourself which will make you have no time to criticise others.
15. To be too large to worry, too noble for anger, too strong for fear and too happy to permit the presence of evil.
16. To do the greatest good to the greatest number of people.
17. To live so well that those who come across you will never remain the same.

18. To think well of yourself and to proclaim this fact to the world, not in loud words, but in good deeds.

These are wonderful and powerful goals that everyone of us involved in the ministry must strive for everyday. I must confess that they are what I am striving for and they are my lifelong objectives. They have helped me in no small measure to move forward. I have not got to where I want, but I am happy to report that I have left where I was before!. When you grow in them, your church and ministry will grow.

Pastor's Price For Church Growth 8

"There is a key to the growth of your church, find it out from God"
- *Francis Bola Akin - John.*

It is one thing to be convinced that church growth is alright but it is quite another to see it actually occur. Church growth is usually not automatic, it takes doing. The major purpose of this book is to help you, as a church leader, understand as thoroughly as possible just what you need to do if your church is going to grow to its full potential.

True, there are some rare situations where the harvest is so ripe that churches will grow almost no matter what. Pastors of those churches seem to break all the rules, ignore church growth principles, and still see their churches grow.

Yet we will need to know how to lead a church to growth and the prices we will need to pay so that growth can be kept on course and obstacles to growth can be dealt with and removed. Growing churches still need to learn church growth principles so that the growth can be sustained and the future of the church secured.

To lead the church to growth, the Pastor is very important. The first principle of church growth says; "The Pastor must want the church to grow and be willing to pay the price.

In this chapter, I will be enumerating the prices the Pastor must pay for the growth of the church. However, let us first examine three salient principles that cannot be compromised if growth must be seen.

PASTOR AS A LEADER IN THE CHURCH

A strong leader is needed if the church is to grow. One of the greatest problem of the African church is leadership. It has done much havoc to the extent that I have included it as one of the diseases that hinders growth in the church. I have named it - Leadmania, meaning the leadership that leads to digression of everything that is good and worthwhile in the church.

If churches are going to maximise their growth potentials, they need Pastors who are strong and dynamic leaders. As a leader, the Pastor must serve, show love and concern to his people. He must be a good example and a role model, then the people will joyfully accept and follow his leadership.

He should be authoritative without being authoritarian. He should dictate without being a dictator. He must communicate and share. He must be in the front leading, but not too far from his people. He will then be able to inspire confidence in his people and they in turn will be proud of his leadership.

I must admit that the type of leadership I have been describing is few and far between in many churches of today. Rather, what we see are polarised, suspicious, poor, assertive, non-communicating, crooked, twisting, haphazard, spasmodic, self-aggrandising and position conscious leadership. The more reason the health and well -being of many churches are greatly jeopardised.

Growth in churches demand good, effective and inspiring leadership. It is non-negotiable. In most churches, especially denominational churches, the Pastor only holds the title and position, he is not the real leader. The actual leadership is in the hand of some lay leaders. Growth will be a mirage in such churches until the Pastor prove to be a true leader.

PASTOR AS A COACH

One of the most formidable obstacle to church growth is the idea that only the clergy can do the work of the ministry and the people as shareholders have done their part as long as they pay their financial dues.

In churches where these view hold sway, growth will almost be impossible. Growth is possible when the Pastor is allowed to function in his scriptural role of coaching, training and equipping the saints for the work of the ministry. He sets the goal, communicates it and properly motivates the people toward the goal attainment through discovering and developing God's gift in their lives.

> If churches are going to maximise their growth potentials, they need Pastors who are strong and dynamic leaders

To truly see growth in the church, the Pastor must function as a coach. He must be a developer of people. He must harness the gifts of the people.

The growth of the church in this end time demands that the Pastor functions more and more as a coach than just being a shepherd. As a shepherd, it will be difficult for the church to cross the 200 membership barrier. When the Pastor functions as a coach and the people accept to do their own part of playing the game, definitely the goal of growth will be realized.

PASTORAL LONGEVITY

Studies have reinforced the positive balance between ministerial longevity and church growth. It is not until a minister have served for 3-5 years in his church that a bias towards growth becomes apparent.

The first year is usually a honeymoon year and only in the second or third year would he have familiarised himself enough with his new environment and then his programmes for growth can be imbibed and accepted.

Pastors with 'Destination Disease' - who are usually and always on the move or looking for greener pastures rarely see growth in their churches. Pastors must see their churches as God's place for them, and make a long term commitment, only then will growth be experienced.

It needs to be recognized that the pattern of short-term pastoring is relatively something new. Pastors need to recognise the fact that there are two ways to get a larger church. Either you move to another one or stay where you are and lead the present church to growth.

> To truly see growth in the church, the Pastor must function as a coach. He must be a developer of people. He must harness the gifts of the people

Denominations should take cognizance of this fact and as much as possible do the transfer and postings of their Pastors in the light of this truth.

PASTOR'S PRICE FOR GROWTH

Nothing comes cheap. Any worthwhile achievement comes at great cost. Therefore, there are special prices that a Pastor must pay to lead a church to growth.

The Bible says in Luke 14:28; **"Which of you, intending to build a tower does not sit down first and count the cost?..."**. Since church growth is not easy and cheap, Pastors must ask themselves before making plans for growth this salient question; - Am I willing to pay the price?

I shall now proceed to describe the prices one after the other:

A.   **Accepting Responsibility for Growth:**

This is too much a price to pay for many Pastors that profess to desire church growth. They would rather blame everybody for the non-growth. They would look for scape-goats than accept the fact of their failure to grow. They prefer to fix the blame than to fix the problem.

Growth demands that responsibility for growth must be accepted by the Pastor. He sets the priorities, vision and areas of change. He is responsible for the results. But too many Pastors want authority and not accountability.

Reasons why Pastors don't want to accept responsibility for growth are:

1. It involves a great risk - risk of failure
2. They are fearful of growth
3. They are not growth - conscious
4. Most are not given the free hand to function
5. They are largely ignorant of what to do.

B. **Hard Work:**

The ministry is such a place that it is easy to become indolent and self-indulging. Nobody is watching over your shoulders to force you to your duties. Therefore it is better to remain in the status quo and be satisfied than to aspire to grow because growth means hard and serious work.

A common trait of Pastors of growing churches is their strong work habits. They are not lazy men, they work hard, and their churches reflect their efforts.

Areas of work

1. **Prayer and Serious Fasting:**

The first area the Pastor must work very hard is engaging in serious times of fasting and praying. For quite sometime, the importance and necessity of waiting upon the Lord in terms of fasting and praying has been largely underplayed. Due recognition has not been given to this heavenly blessed exercise. It has been tossed to a corner, yet growth cannot take a strong footing in the church if fasting and prayers are neglected.

Argentina, Korea and China are the flash points of great growth of the kingdom of God in the world today. One of the reasons is that saints in these Countries have resolved to draw down the hand of God through fasting and prayers.

Strong prayer and fasting base must be built in the church if great growth will be seen. Fasting and prayer of varying lengths of time must be constantly and continuously embarked upon by the church to secure open heaven for great growth.

> Fasting and prayer of varying lengths of time must be constantly and continuously embarked upon by the church to secure open heaven for great growth

The Pastor must set the example in this regard and lead his people to fast and pray in these eight areas suggested by David Branyt:

> They should fast **SCRIPTURALLY** - Matt. 9:15
> They should fast **SENSIBLY** - Acts 10:30
> They should fast **SECRETLY** - Matt. 6:16-18.

They should fast **SENSITIVELY** - Acts 13:1-13.
They should fast **SYSTEMATICALLY** - Matt. 6:16
They should fast **SACRIFICIALLY** - Isa. 58:6,12
They should fast **SPECIFICALLY** - Isa. 58:6
They should fast **SUPERNATURALLY** - Acts 13:2,3.

Wherever the church is growing today in the world, it is the working of the Holy Spirit in answer to the prayers and fasting of His people. Without much prayer and fasting we cannot see the growth we are desiring.

One of the factors responsible for the spectacular growth of The Redeemed Christian Church of God in Nigeria is their usual practise of long periods of fasting. It is arguably the fastest growing church in Nigeria today.

In 1995-96 they planted over 342 churches, by 1996-97 they planted over 540 thriving churches and they also set the goal of planting 4,000 lively churches in the year 1997-98. I am happy to report that the goal was wonderfully achieved and by year 2000, the church had attained its stated goal of having 5 million members.

The commitment to serious prayer and fasting is one of the factors that we cannot ignore in this spectacular growth.

The Pastor that desires growth must be ready to practise serious fasting and prayer with his people. It is a price that must be unflinchingly paid.

2. **Visiting and Studying Growing Churches:**

A Yoruba adage says "He that doesn't get to another man's farm will think his own is the biggest". This holds true in the area of church growth. Visiting and studying other growing churches will inspire and enlighten you. You will be able to see what God is doing through others and thereby receive challenges to do more.

The purpose of such visit is not to criticise and find fault, nor to adopt everything the visited church is doing hook, line and sinker, but to observe how things are being done in ways that enable sinners to respond to the gospel more effectively. This will help us to review and revise some of the ways we have been doing church, which have rather proved ineffective.

I am aware that many Pastors don't go out, they believe there is nothing new to learn out there. Pastors who fall into this category are some of the most backward I have ever seen in the ministry!

3. **Taking Courses in Church Growth:**

The mushrooming of Bible Colleges and Seminaries in the last few years have not had the desired impact upon the church in Nigeria and Africa generally. Many of them have little or nothing to say on church growth. Their graduates have not been able to see much growth because they are hardly exposed to growth teachings.

The few that care enough to include Church Growth in their curriculum do so grudgingly, erroneously thinking that it is only a course subject.

However, a new day is dawning and many are making frantic search for answers to years of barrenness and fruitlessness. They don't have to search too far, our school: **International Institute of Church Growth** has got the courses to help them. It offers non-theological but practical courses on growth in the church.

The Institute was established in March 1996 with the aim of helping the growth and health of the church. In its over nine years of existence, the Institute has trained over 1,500 Pastors and church leaders with attendant growth testimonies.

Pastors that desire growth will do well to take a Growth course in this pioneering Institute in order to have a better grasp of Church Growth principles and how it works in the African context.

You can know more about the school by visiting our office or call any of our telephone lines for further information. You will never regret coming to the school.

4. **Attending Church Growth Seminars and Conferences:**

The Church Growth Pastor must be ready to partake, attend and benefit from seminars and conferences being organised on Church Growth.

In reality, Church Growth seminars and conferences are few and far between until recently. Many being organised are too shallow in real growth information and materials, yet Pastors that desire growth must find out the one they will benefit from and attend.

Seminars and conferences provide opportunity for sharing, interaction and learning new methods and better ways of doing ministry.

5. **Training and Developing Workers:**

This is one area where the majority of churches in Nigeria and Africa find difficult to handle. Not much premium is placed on the training and development of workers. Largely, the workers are neglected, untrained but expected to function effectively. The few churches that believe in it do it haphazardly.

Many Pastors are bereft of ideas and lack materials to train their workers. The more reason the workers cannot really support the vision of the Pastor. Not much can be achieved without the cooperative efforts of the

> The church cannot really grow without the people taking active part and using their God-given gifts and talents

people.

The church cannot really grow without the people taking active part and using their God-given gifts and talents. But if they are not trained and developed, growth will be a mirage.

The craze among churches now is starting Bible Schools after some measure of growth. As good as this may sound, it is not the most important thing. Institute of training for discovering and developing of the talents, gifts and ministries of the people is the most important.

The Pastor must pour out himself into his people and then they will rise up to grow the church. We must develop the people that will develop the church.

6. **Function as Agent of Change:**

Change is the only constant thing in life. Stagnant and declining churches view change with alarm because they are so set in their ways. They have built many alibis and myths against the growth of the church.

Some non-growth philosophies such as;

1. Remnant theology,
2. Glorification of littleness,
3. Faithfulness versus success - the believe that God has not called us to be successful but to be faithful.

4. Holier - than - thou notion that often reason that why sinners are not joining the church is because of our higher standard of holiness and teaching.
5. Maintenance culture - which gives the idea that if we maintain the saints inside, they will naturally reach out to their neighbours.

These growth restricting theologies must be reviewed and changed by the Pastor if growth is to be seen in the church. The price of change must be paid by the Pastor that desires growth. Though, change must not be done for the sake of change.

The four steps to effective change that would result in great achievement in the church are:

>Plan purposefully
>Prepare prayerfully
>Proceed positively and
>Pursue persistently.

C. **Share the Vision:**

The role of vision in the growth and well-being of the church cannot be over-emphasised. In reality, vision has not been stressed enough in Church Growth teachings.

Without vision the church's purpose or direction cannot achieve anything worthwhile or long-lasting. A church without vision has been likened to a car without fuel, lacking the necessary ingredient. Also, like a wedding without the bride; missing the most essential element.

The Pastor must get the vision of God for the church through seeking and waiting upon the Lord. He must discover God's mind and purpose for the church, then share and communicate the vision to the people. The vision of:

> People commit themselves more deeply to a vision than to a personality

a. **Who we are**:- Why we are different from others, our peculiarities and special ministry emphasis must be known by the people.

b. **Where we are going**:- What we want to achieve and accomplish. The people we want to impact and affect must be known.

c. **How do we get there**:- The plans, goal and strategies must be shared with the people.

These areas must be specifically defined and realistic. It must be embraced and owned by the people. If they detest, oppose and reject the vision, it cannot be fulfilled. For the people to embrace and own the vision, it must be effectively communicated by the Pastor. The Pastor must say it simply, often and model it so that the people can catch the vision.

Every opportunity must be used to communicate the vision, such as the pulpit, bulletins, printouts, leaders meetings and the likes. People commit themselves more deeply to a vision than to a personality. It is the church driven by God-given vision that can grow and flourish.

D.   **Share the Ministry:**

There is this story of a Pastor who believes that he is indispensable to his church. He believes he is the life and blood of the church. He therefore was in the habit of doing everything in the church.

He will single-handedly do all the preaching, teaching, administration, counselling, committee-meeting, visitation, follow-up activities, and things moved on to a certain point.

Then one day, he had cause to travel out of town for an urgent meeting which will last for two weeks.

While away, he was constantly phoning the wife to enquire as to the state of affairs of the church. The wife reported that things were bad and upside down since he left. The Pastor was happy with this situation report because according to him, it shows his indispensability to the church!

Well, his work is dying in his presence. If things could turned upside down, in just two weeks of his absence, what will happen if he suddenly died?

The lesson in the story is that the church has no future without a shared ministry. One of the marks of a great minister is the percentage of the lay people that are involved in the ministry in his church.

The diagram below shows two basic types of Pastors:

1. Carrying the Church   2. On top of the church

Diagram (1) shows the Pastor labouring under the burden of the church. He is carrying the church and therefore is under intense pressure and the demands on him by the church is becoming unbearable.

This is the situation of Pastors that don't believe in sharing the ministry. Sadly, they oftentimes are crushed by the weight of the church.

Diagram (2) shows the Pastor standing on top of the church. He is not under any particular pressure because he believes and practise the art of sharing the ministry and delegation of authority.

The people serve as the extension arm of his

ministry. He does the most important aspect of the ministry and delegate the rest to his people. He functions as an equipper, a coach and a supervisor.

While the first Pastor cannot grow beyond 100-150 in membership, the second Pastor has unlimited possibilities for growth.

Here are reasons why Pastors don't share the ministry:

- Pastors are not trained to equip people to minister
- Pastors are not expected to work through people
- Pastors receive ego satisfaction from Messiah status
- Equipping people is hard work.
- They believe their subordinates will not be able to-handle the assignment.
- They fear competition from subordinates.
- They are afraid of losing recognition
- They are fearful that their weaknesses will be exposed
- They feel they won't have the time to turn over the work and provide the necessary training.
- Dearth of good resources for training.

It is not hard to see why sharing the ministry is too high a price to pay for some Pastors who want growth.

However, if the people are not ready to partake

in the ministry and are not willing to minister within the church, there is usually a **LEAD** problem.

Leadership problem
Exposure problem
Attitude problem
Discipleship problem.

The task of a true and great leader is to train the people to do the work even better than himself until God gets the glory.

These and many more are the prices the Pastor who desires growth in his church must unflinchingly pay. He cannot do otherwise.

Rapid growth is good and exciting, but solid and lasting growth takes time. One will outlast the other.

Many churches have seen growth without their Pastors knowing, let alone practise all that have been written here, yet a cursory look will reveal that their growth will sooner or later fizzle away. And the church will encounter many avoidable troubles and bottlenecks. But when these areas are clearly known, imbibed and practised, by the time the growth starts it will be durable and sustainable.

> The task of a true and great leader is to train the people to do the work even better than himself until God gets the glory

The Pastor And His Co-workers 9

The first principle of Church Growth is that the Pastor must want the church to grow and be willing to pay the price. So also the people must want the church to grow and be willing to pay the price.

It is pertinent therefore for Pastors to take note of how to choose and how not to choose people who are to be co-workers with them in the ministry.

RIGHT WAYS OF CHOOSING CO-WORKERS

1. **By the character and not just the ability of the person:**

    It is unfortunate that many leaders have emphasized the gift, ability and talent more than character in choosing workers in the church. And this has resulted in many problems in the church today. But if the leader is to follow the Biblical way of choosing his co-labourers, he should choose by character.

Co-labourers should be chosen based on strong spiritual and godly character. Their lives must testify and be an example for others to follow.

In choosing his co-workers the leader should follow the example of the first Apostles in Acts 6:1-3 who based the qualifications of those to be chosen as co-workers on their spiritual characters.

2. **After much prayer and seeking God:**

The Pastor who is willing to succeed in his ministry must choose his co-labourers after much prayer and seeking of God's face.

Here, the example of the Lord provides us a clue (Luke 6:12-16). We could see the Lord of glory Himself seeking the Father for a whole night before choosing His twelve Apostles. He did not take the liberty of choosing by Himself without the consent of His heavenly Father.

If our Lord and Master did pray and sought God's face before choosing His followers, who are we that we would not do the same? History proved right the choice the Master made. So also is the Pastor who wish to succeed.

3. **After examining others' feelings about the individual:**

This is a very important point, failure to abide by this point in choosing co-workers have ruined the ministry of many Pastors. They chose those who are contemptuous in the peoples' eyes and those who have grave question marks hanging on their lives and that has brought an end to the ministry.

But the Pastor who is willing to succeed in his ministry must take heed to this point. Paul the Apostle realized the importance of this point and he told Timothy to remember it while choosing his leaders (I Timothy 3:7).

The Apostles also did not fail to take cognizance of it. (Acts 6:3). Those to be chosen to a position of honour must have good report of the people both within and without.

4. **By their dedication to Jesus Christ:**

This may well be the reason why many workers handle the Lord's work with levity and unconcerned attitudes today. Because they are not dedicated to the Lord of the work, therefore they can do the work as they pleased and saw fit. But this

> Workers must be chosen to positions of trust by the virtue of their dedication to the Lord Jesus Christ

should not be so.

Workers must be chosen to positions of trust by the virtue of their dedication to the Lord Jesus Christ. If they are not dedicated to Christ, the work cannot prosper in their hands and everything will be stagnant. But if they are dedicated and are serious followers of Jesus Christ, the work must inevitably prosper in their hands.

Therefore, a Pastor who wants success with His co-labourers must choose those to work with him on the basis of their dedication and devotion to Jesus Christ.

5. By their specific Ministry and Calling:

Many times this point is overlooked by many Pastors. They only choose men into positions without consideration for their ministries and calling.

It is the clear example of putting round pegs in square holes. But the Pastor who is desiring success in the ministry must follow the command in Romans 12:6-8; that every one must abide by the ministry which he had been given. It is then that success will come. But this will not be possible if the Pastor did not have the ability to see the specific ministry of every potential co-worker.

6. By their love for lost souls:

The potential co-labourer must be someone

who have this quality, else, he will only be working just for the sake of appointment. But if there is the passion for lost souls and desire to win them to Christ, the shared goal of the Pastor and the co-workers will be achieved.

When this passion for souls is present, the worker will be willing to go through anything in order to win others for Christ. For the Pastor to realize and fulfill his ministry, he must choose those who have this passion and love for lost souls. It is then that the work will be easy and success will be achieved.

7.   By their love for God's people:

One will be inviting failure into his ministry by choosing those who did not exhibit love for the people of God.

No progress or success will be recorded in the ministry of a Pastor who chose as co-workers those who do not love the people of God.

If such are chosen, they are not co-labourers, rather they are hireling (John 10:12). Because they will not care for the sheep, they will only be concerned with their own belly and satisfaction and the wolves will carry the sheep away in their presence.

Therefore, if the Pastor desires success and does not want to lose any of his sheep, he should choose those who have the love of the sheep at heart.

8. **By their willingness to serve when unnoticed:**

It is dangerous to choose as co-labourers those who have the love for praise and position. They cannot seek for the growth of the work, but for their own popularity and opportunity to cave a niche for themselves. Such people cannot work as co-labourers with a Pastor.

But those who are willing to serve when unnoticed and who could labour on what they are not praised or referred to should be chosen as co-labourers by the Pastor who wishes not to have problems with the sheep and success of his shepherding ministry.

> When the ability of a person is the only yardstick used in selecting him into a position of co-labouring with the Pastor, the inevitable result will be the ruin and destruction of that ministry

Diothrephes is a clear example of the kind of problem this type of people who are not willing to serve unnoticed will give to the sheep and the ministry of the Pastor (III John 9,10).

9. **By their unity of Spirit:**

Since it is clear that 'two cannot walk together

except they agree', the Pastor will only be looking for problems and crisis in his pastoral ministry if he should choose those who do not possess the unity of Spirit. The devil will gain access into the sheep's fold and the wolf will have a field-day in destroying the sheep if the co-labourers are those who are not in unity of spirit with the Pastor.

But if those who possess this quality are chosen, the work will be easier for the shepherd and the sheep will also grow.

WRONG WAYS OF CHOOSING CO-WORKERS

1.   **On ability and not character:**

A Pastor should not choose by ability, but by character. He should not put anyone into position as his co-labourers on the basis of his ability alone.

Failure on this wise have led to the ruin of many ministries and the sheep wounded and scattered. When the ability of a person is the only yardstick used in selecting him into a position of co-labouring with the Pastor, the inevitable result will be the ruin and destruction of that ministry.

Such a person who is without character but only ability will not mind to harass the sheep and abuse them in his fleshly and ungodly ways. Therefore a Pastors should not choose those who are going to be his co-workers based on their ability alone.

2. **When under pressure to fill a position in the church:**

It is sad and unfortunate that this is the vogue today in churches. The Pastors only choose people to fill positions when they are under pressure.

They only want 'position occupants. They do not care who he is and what he will or can do, but just to fill the position with somebody. But this should not be so. Pastors must never choose when they are under pressure to fill a position in the church. But they should wait to consider the person who is fit for the position only.

> Every good and faithful Pastor who wishes to succeed must not compromise the standard

This is more pertinent because once someone is put into a position, to remove the person is not always easy. Therefore, care should be taken by the pastor who wishes to succeed in his ministry not to choose of co-labourers when under pressure.

3. **When you must compromise your own standards or the standards of God's word:**

It is an ominous sign and a source of concern to

earliest Christians, that compromise has entered into the pulpits today. And nowhere is this visible than in the manner workers are being chosen in churches.

The ungodly Elders, who are like Eli the prophet whom the Lord had forsaken will pressurise the Pastor to compromise the standard of the word of God in the choosing of some certain people into position - because they are their favorites and pet children in the church.

Though it is clear to all and sundry that such people are tragically unworthy for such positions yet this 'old prophets' will pressurise the Pastor to compromise the standard of God's word by putting such people into the coveted position. May God save us! Every good and faithful Pastor who wishes to succeed and desires the presence of the Lord in his ministry must not compromise the standard. He must stoutly refuse to bow down to the wishes of those who want him to compromise the standard of the word in the area of choosing of co-workers.

4. **Because they give a lot of money to the church:**

This is the general practise in churches today, and one of the strongest reasons people adduced as a criterion for choosing workers in the church. But that is not the way to choose co-labourers.

The Pastor must never allow money to be the factor on which he would base the appointment of his co-labourers, else those with the large sums of money will eventually dominate and begin to dictate to him because, they will claim that they had the largest donation in the church and thereby they should have strong say in the affairs of the church.

This should never be so in the church of God. And in order to forestall such embarrassing situations, the Pastor must not choose co-labourers on the premises of giving money to the church.

5. **Because they are academically sound**

This is another area of common mistakes in the body of Christ today. People, though they are glaringly and spiritually unqualified for the post, are chosen on the basis that they have the most academic education in the church.

> People with competitive nature are dangerous and inimical for the growth and well-being of the ministry of the Pastor

Though, education is good and desirable, yet, it must never be placed above sound and strong spiritual character in our consideration of those to be chosen as co-labourers in God's vineyard. Even though God has not put a premium on ignorance, yet he does not base His selection on academic qualifications only. This trend must however be reversed in the church today if the Pastor desires to see God at work in his ministry.

It is sad to say that it is these knowledgeable and learned fellows but, who are unspiritual that go about troubling and causing crisis in the churches today.

The Pastor who really desires success must therefore not choose by academic qualifications alone, but also by spirituality, godliness and maturity in the faith.

6. **Because they are young and have much talent and energy:**

Choosing co-workers on the basis of this point will augment the growth of the ministry nor the young peoples' lives.

Though the young should not be discouraged, but rather encouraged to be alive for the Lord, yet they must not be chosen solely on the basis of their youthfulness, talents or energy, but on the basis of the depth of their character coupled with these talents and energy.

7. **Because they threaten to leave the Church if you do not use them immediately:**

These are the set of people who should never be put into positions in the church as long as they have such attitude. They are always the trouble makers. And failure to heed this advice of not choosing such will inevitably result in regret and problems in the church.

Such people that clamour for position immediately they are around should never be chosen. If they decide to leave the church, they should be allowed to leave, because their continued presence will only bring trouble for the church.

8. **Because they have competitive nature in other areas:**

This should never be considered as a factor in choosing of co-workers by the pastor. People with competitive nature are dangerous and inimical for the growth and well-being of the ministry of the Pastor. Since we are not doing our own work, there is no justification in competing with others.

The Lord has committed different works or assignment into our hands and everyone should strive only to fulfill the part that had been committed into his hand.

By appointing people with competitive nature or spirit into position, one will be inviting jealousy, infighting, bickering and envy among his co-workers which will not be in the best interest of the ministry or the church.

HOW PASTORS SHOULD TRAIN THEIR CO-WORKERS

1. **By Giving them Direction and not Confusion:**

A leader should constantly be at the front so that he can give to his co-workers a sense of direction and guidance. He should co-ordinate and direct them in a manner that will make him win their respect. He should train them by directing them with wisdom in order to achieve the shared goal. He should train them in a manner that gives them confidence and not confusion. Anything that might bring confusion to them must be tacitly avoided.

2. **By Giving them Encouragement and not Condemnation:**

A leader must be the most optimistic person. A pessimist never make a leader. Since it is the lot of the leader to train his co-workers, he should take utmost care in this venture. He should make sure that he encourages his co-labourers.

This is one of the most effective ways of training co-labourers. By encouraging

> The leader should also create the atmosphere whereby the co-labourers do their respective work with the joy of service

them, the co-workers will be able to develop their gifts, abilities and confidence in the area they are placed.

When they experience failure, the usual practice is to condemn, but a good leader will lend support and encouragement. He will make them realize that such failure is not final, but that they should rise up and try again.

By using encouragement and not condemnation as a means of training, the Pastor will be able to produce loyal and faithful co-labourers who will be at their best.

3. **By Giving them Service and not Servitude:**

The workers should not feel that they are under a taskmaster. The leader should not be domineering or be a dictator over his co-labourers. They should not have the slightest feeling that they are under a servitude.

The Pastor should create a conducive atmosphere of service as a means of training for his co-labourers and not servitude. He should be willing to release them to areas of service that they are best suited in order to develop their capabilities. The leader should also create the atmosphere whereby the co-labourers do their respective work with the joy of service. They should be able to find joy in doing the work they are assigned, it is then that they are not under servitude.

4. **By Giving them Inspiration and not Negation:**

A leader should never negate or hold in light esteem those who are his co-workers. There should be no feeling of negation by the workers toward their Pastor.

The Pastor should try always to inspire them to service. He should be a worthy example to them. He must be a burning and a shining light unto them, and a constant source of inspiration both by action and words to those he hopes to train for high achievement.

It is by giving them inspiration and challenge that he can bring out the best in them. Their contributions to the work by their service or suggestions should never be negated, but praised and rewarded.

5. **By Giving them Discipline and not Disconcern:**

Discipline is a vital part of the church. A leader who wishes to keep to the standard must be prepared to administer loving but faithful discipline on his co-workers.

If there is no discipline for those who erred, the rest might follow such ways later, but if they are faithfully disciplined, then the rest will take a cue and desist from such ways in the future.

In administering the discipline, the interest and

welfare of the offender must be taken into consideration and kept at heart. It must be done with their restoration in view.

There must be concern in the way and manner we administer discipline to workers that have erred. The offenders must be able to read love and concern for their welfare in us as we lovingly, but faithfully administer the right measure of punishment for the offence committed.

> The way events, occurrences and situations are being handled in the church goes a long way either to give hope or despair to the workers

6. **By Giving them Channel and not Control:**

The Pastor who desires to train his workers for maximum production must abide by this timely principle. He must give them channel to flow through and not to limit them on the extent to which they can flow or develop.

They must not be put into a 'strait jacket' or a 'stereotype' control that will hamper their seriousness and calculated risks for growth in their various assignments. They should be given guidelines and then left to develop and expand on their own.

7. By Giving them Release and not Bondage:

The workers must feel free and relaxed in the presence of their leaders. They should feel free to express their ideas and make whatever contributions they have for the work.

The leader who does not have his workers in such a state is seriously lacking in his leadership. And urgent steps to rectify such situation must be embarked upon immediately.

The workers who feel that they are in bondage and cannot express their views cannot work with maximum efficiency. They should be released for their various ministries and not held in bondage to man-made rules or regulations.

8. By Giving them Hope and not Despair:

The good leader or pastor should as much as possible try to give hope and not despair to his workers. The situation of things might not be encouraging, but the handling of such situations should be a source of hope to the workers that better days are coming.

The way events, occurrences and situations are being handled in the church goes a long way either to give hope or despair to the workers. If such events are handled in a way that leave much to be desired, then the inevitable result is that the workers will be discouraged and if such situation persists, then despair will set in and the work will grind to almost a halt.

But things should be done in a way that will give hope and joy to the workers, for it is then that they will persist and determine to do more, even in the face of seeming impossibilities.

HOW PASTORS SHOULD WORK WITH THEIR CO-WORKERS

1. By recognizing his own ministry strengths:

This is a very important point. The Pastor should evaluate and see where his ministry strengths, lie. He should be able to recognize the areas where he is strongest. He should know where his strength and power are and then concentrate on those areas.

By recognizing his strong areas and concentrating on harnessing those power and strengths the leader will be bidding for more success in his ministry.

This was what the Apostles did concerning Peter and John. They realized that they had the gift of laying of hands and others will receive the Baptism in the Holy Ghost. They had to send them to Samaria (Acts 8:14-17) to minister to those who have newly been saved and needed this experience. Peter and John's ministry strengths were recognized and they were harnessed.

2. **By recognizing his own ministry limitations and weaknesses:**

It is unfortunate that many so called leaders are not willing to admit this point today. They tend to paint the picture of an 'all in all' leader, who can do everything. But this will not speak well for the well being of the ministry and the leader.

A leader should recognize his limitations and weaknesses. When he has recognized this he should then choose workers who are strong in those areas so that things can be balanced up.

This was what Moses did, when, through the wise counsel of Jethro, he recognized his own limitation, and chose workers that can do the work well as he could. No leader can do it all, and God has placed under the leader, co-workers who can compliment and help in his weak areas.

3. **By recognizing other Members' Strengths:**

In order for the work to move on as it should, the leader should recognize other members strengths and abilities. God has not placed any useless member in his church.

> God has not placed any useless member in his church

Others' capabilities and potentials should be recognized and they should be placed where they can best use these strengths for God's glory. If they are not recognized and used, they will stand afar off and criticize the leader. But if their strengths are recognized and harnessed they will be part of the ministry.

4. **By Maintaining a Servant Heart and Spirit:**

A leader should not be proud. He should not show any attitude of "I am great, you are small" to his co-labourers. He should maintain a servant's heart at all times. He should serve them and be a perfect example unto them. He should also be able to come to their level.

5. **By having Inter-personal Involvement with one Another:**

The leader should not be too far ahead of his workers. He should be able to come to their standards and be able to relate well with them. Having activities together should be encouraged.

The workers' well-being should be the utmost concern to the leader. Both the leader and co-labourers should be interested in one another. Each should be interested in one another's success. Christ's view of His Kingdom was that of a community of members serving one another.

6. **By Maintaining a Family Spirit in the Team:**

Here, we find the example of the Master very instructive. It was said that those who came to arrest

Him could not differentiate between Him and His disciples and Judas had to reveal Him by kissing Him.

He was so identified with the disciples and maintained a family spirit. He made them feel at home in His presence. So must leaders of today do with co-labourers. They must be united together and a cordial family atmosphere cultivated at all times. There should be natural family love and care for one another.

7. **By Cultivating Loyalty and Trust in the Team:**

The leader should be able to trust his workers. When an assignment had been given, they should be made to feel the trust and backing of the leader. And when such is the case, they will be loyal to the leader.

"Writing of his association with Dr. John R. Mott, Paul Super said: "One of my greatest resources these ten years in Poland is the sense of his backing. My greatest pride is his belief in me. Surely one of my greatest motives is to be worthy of his support and to measure up to his expectations of me".

8. **By Maintaining and Encouraging a Forgiving Spirit:**

Blunders and mistakes are inevitable in corianders. And the way the leader handle such mistakes and blunders will go a long way in helping or ruining his co-workers.

The leader should be able to overlook and

forgive the little mistakes of others. He should manifest forgiving spirit at all times, and by so doing will be encouraging the rest member of the team to follow suit with one another.

> An open and honest attitude will speak for the well being of the whole set up

9. **By Cultivating an Honest and Open Attitude with the Team:**

There should be no dishonest in the leader. Any step that require explanation should be explained. Any matter that need clarification must be so done.

An open and honest attitude will speak for the well being of the whole set up. It is always good that the leader should maintain such attitude. Matters should be discussed freely. Nothing of importance that concerns their welfare or work should be allowed to be shrouded in mystery. Everything must be brought to the fore.

10. **By Maintaining a Teachable Spirit:**

The leader must have such spirit in abundance. He should be willing to learn from his juniors and seniors alike. He cannot be right at all times and should therefore be able to accept others' views and suggestions and implement them. He should admit when he is wrong.

He should be willing to listen to others, and should not feel any tinge of jealousy when God is correcting or leading him through one of the least recognized worker.

11. By Maintaining Good Communication:

This is prime essential in the ministry. No chance must be given to communication break-down. Good communication must be encouraged and preserved. It should be jealously guarded. The devil must not be given a chance here. The workers must feel free to express their mind without harassment. The leader must communicate with workers in a way that shows respect and reverence.

In closing, it remains to be said that the church has always prospered most when it has been blessed with strong and spiritual leaders who expected and experienced the touch of the supernatural in their service.

Therefore, it is the binding duty of those in positions of leadership to face up to the situation and do all that is in their power to see that the touch of a truly biblical and spiritual leadership is passed on to the younger men.

Alphabets Of Achievement   10

> "No church has grown enough, there is always room for growth and improvement"
> - *Francis Bola Akin - John*

We have now come to the last chapter of this book. Because I want to end this book on the upbeat side is the reason I have chosen this topic for the last chapter.

We have gone through many great truths regarding the growth of the church in particular and in relation to the personality of the Pastor.

The tendency is to read all these words and do nothing about them, the more reason we shall jointly consider action verbs that will help you to put all you have learnt into practise. These action words are what will set the right mood and motivation for you to move from mediocrity to marvellous achievement.

Attitude:

Attitude is very important to the progress or otherwise of our lives. Your altitude in life depends on your attitude. Reject negative attitude and embrace the positive one.

Without positive attitude you cannot affirm your determination to bring growth to your life and church. Without the right attitude you cannot affirm and without positive affirmation there can't be achievement. You cannot rise higher than your attitude will allow. By having the right attitude you can turn adversity into achievement.

Believe:

The right attitude will lead you to believe you can do it and that it can happen. You can grow, your church and ministry can experience unlimited growth too. Strong belief is very important to achieving great and spectacular growth in any endeavour.

Mark 9:23; says **"Jesus said unto him, if thou can believe, all things are possible to him that believeth"**. Do you believe in growth, progress and achievement? Then go for it. Your strong believe will open the door for you to fly and not fail. Your believe is you. You cannot attain and achieve more than your believe. Believe you are a failure and you are right.

Believe you can grow and it will happen.

Commit:

Your strong believe in the theology of growth should lead to actual commitment. Until you are committed, your success will be put in abeyance.

Make a commitment to your vision of bringing growth to your church. Until you are committed there is tendency to draw back. The point of commitment is the point of success or failure. Burn your bridges behind you and move on to stupendous growth and blessing.

Desire:

Nothing can quench the fire of deep, insatiable hunger and desire to grow and move forward. The problem with many is that their desire is not strong enough to warrant them to go for their cherished dream.

Your desire must be strong enough to make you to dare and take a calculated risk. God does not bless wishes, He only blesses desires. The desires of the righteous shall be granted. Dare to move forward. Dare to rise up from inertia and fear of failure. Dare to take bold step toward growth and attainment.

The scripture says powerfully in Psalm 37:4; **"Delight thyself in the LORD, and He shall give thee the desire of thine heart".**

What do you desire? Is your desire strong enough to make you to dare and take the step to growth? Remember, beginning is winning because, at least, you would have won over inertia and fear of failure.

Educate, Excel:

> Without the right attitude you cannot affirm and without positive affirmation there can't be achievement

Many who view education as exorbitant should try the cost of ignorance! You will need to educate yourself either formally or informally. You can't possibly know everything, but someone, somewhere is having the knowledge you need to bring untold success into your life. You will need to find the person out. You will need to be humble to learn if you are going to excel. Books, Newspapers, Magazines and Journals contain valuable information that will help you in achieving excellence.

Commitment to excellence demands that you educate yourself in every possible way. Remember this salient truth; Every leader is a learner. When you stop learning you stop leading. If you don't read others nobody will read you. If you stop hearing others, people will stop hearing you, so take step to educate yourself in order to excel.

Find, Faith:

Find God's purpose for your life, ministry, church and then have the faith to pursue it. Faith in God is very necessary for any worthwhile attainment. Everything is possible to the one who have faith. Opposition and obstacles will melt in the presence of strong, indomitable faith and persistence.

Fear of failure and fear of starting has crippled many from success in life. The only antidote to fear is faith. Faith will drive out fear or fear will drive out faith in your life. I am sure you are going to allow faith to drive out the fear of starting so that your sealed blessing can get to you.

Goals:

Goals are statement of faith. Someone says, "When goals goes growth goes, when growth goes, life goes dead on our hands" Goals are to growth what fuel is to the vehicle. Without goals there is nothing to strive for and nothing to accomplish. Set goals for growth. Give yourself wholly to achieving them.

Setting goals and starting early are two wings of the life that soar. Give your best effort to your goals and you will never be disappointed. Empty yourself with reckless abandon to the realization of your stated goals and you will have cause to smile at the end of the day.

Hope:

"Hope maketh not ashamed" is the powerful declaration of the Scripture (Rom. 5:5). Hope is one of the finest words in the world. Hope is a powerful anchor in the soul. As long as there is hope, your success will surely come.

Life might have dealt you a serious blow but you must never give up. You must not lose hope of a better future. Your hope of a better tomorrow must burn brightly in your heart The storm may blow, the clouds may not give its sunshine and the birds may have gone into hiding because of the storm. Your hope that the storm will pass, the sun will shine and the birds will sing again must never falter.

Imagine:

Someone said; "The me I see is the me I will become". The image you have about yourself is the reality you are going to get. How you see yourself in your mind is very crucial to your accomplishment. Powerful imagination is an effective aid in accomplishing great goals.

Abraham had a poor image of himself until God had

> Every leader is a learner. When you stop learning you stop leading. If you don't lead others nobody will read you

to change his name and the way he viewed himself through counting the stars at night. Through that encounters his image of himself changed forever and he was able to experience the great blessings of God.

Dreams are the language of the Spirit. Imagine success and you will have it. Positive, powerful imagination and dreams are the vehicle of great accomplishments.

Jik out the Junks:

It is your duty to jik out all the junks you have accumulated inside you. Junks are negative thoughts, impossibility thinking, wrong notions, myths and half truths about growth, programmes and expansion. They must be done away with.

Junks in the mind cluster God's inflow. Great ideas and creative insights cannot flow into your heart if these junks are occupying there. Divorce yourself of these junks. Drop them, reject them, disown them and embrace all the positive emotions that will accelerate your growth.

Knock:

Knock out all the opposition that demons can raise against your effort through prayer and fasting. Waiting upon the Lord is the surest way to defeat all the enemies of your growth.

The machinations, activities and crafty

manipulations of demons must be knocked out if the desired growth and attainment must be seen. Don't give place to the devil (Eph. 4:27). Either in your heart, mind, body, church, home and life. Don't give a quarter of an inch to the devil. Always be on the offensive.

Love, Laugh:

Growth of every kind cannot happen if we do not possess a strong and durable love for the Lord. It is our love for the Lord that serves as the strong propeller that would want us to see Him glorified in every way possible. Love for the Lord in the heart would make us to obey and serve Him with all our heart, body, soul and strength. It will enable us to love others and thereby want them to come to Him and know Him as their Lord and Saviour.

Love in our heart would make us offer a ready smile and a hearty laughter with others. Love in the heart cannot be hidden for too long. It would want to help, support, advice and uplift others. Having a hearty laughter will reduce tension and ease up our tensed nerves. Remember your dressing is not complete if you haven't put on a smile.

Make:

Church Growth is not a theory, it is very practical. You must decide to make it happen in your church. Decide and determine to make it happen in your situation.

If you are only interested in maintaining the status quo you will not make any headway. You can do it! It can be done in your church! The decline and years of barrenness can be stopped. Your church can experience turn around.

> It is our love for the Lord that serves as the strong propeller that would want us to see Him glorified in every way possible

Vigorous growth is possible in your church, but it will not happen if you don't decide to make it happen. Get this fact, there is no partiality with God. If He had done it for others He will do it for you. Others are not more favourable than you.

Everybody is born with one sure right. You can succeed in your endeavour. Motivate and mobilize yourself for growth. Be self-starting, kick and prime yourself for growth. Be highly mobilized to make it happen.

Needs:

You can make a headway in any endeavour if you decide to meet the needs of others. If you are willing to help enough people to meet their needs, your own needs will be met. Success is possible when you find a need and meet it.

The fastest growing churches in the world today

are churches that meet the needs of their people. People have two basic kind of needs; felt and real. Their felt needs are comfort, joy, love, healing, deliverance, solution, blessings and prosperity, while their real need is a vibrant relationship with the very Son of God.

Moreover, they will not realize their real need until their felt needs are met. When you do church in such a way as to meet the real and felt needs of people growth, will invariably happen.

Obstacles:

Growth will not come on the platter of gold. Everything may not work according to schedule. The road is going to be rough, tough, narrow and bumpy.

There will be obstacles, oppositions, hindrances and stumbling blocks. Yet you must determine to overcome all that the devil can throw at you. You must pursue and overtake all the hindrances. Your stumbling blocks must become your stepping stones to success. With your gaze fixed on the Saviour, you will overcome every opposition on the way.

Obstacles, oppositions, hindrances and stumbling blocks cannot stand the power of a ready mind and man. They will have to give way or be crumbled under feet. Yes, you can overcome, prevail and grow.

Prayer:

Make prayer your regular habit and God will make miracle regular occurrence for you. Prayer is the mother of all church growth. Church growth is possible when believing prayers are made.

Yonngi Cho declares that "Church growth is 60% prayer and 40% principles and method". Nothing much can be achieved without prayer. Get into the prayer action, commit yourself to prayer and seeking of God's face. Knock out every excuse and complain not to pray.

> The fastest growing churches in the world today are churches that meet the needs of their people

You must also add perseverance to your prayer. Prayer without perseverance is like a boy who pressed a doorbell and the man in the house answered from inside that he was coming, but before the man got to the door the boy had run away.

Pray perseveringly to succeed. The key to success is to plan purposefully, prepare prayerfully, proceed positively and pursue perseveringly.

Quit:

You have heard that winners don't quit and

quitters don't win. The ability to stick to your vision when you are hardest hit is the sure mark of success.

You must be a postage stamp Christian. The postage stamp has the knack of sticking to a thing until it gets there. When you quit, you are lost and forgotten. The mightiest victories come after the severest of battles. Stick and stand by your dream and vision. Rise up and be counted on the side of growth. Hold fast to your dream, don't give it up for any price in the whole world.

Resist:

For you not to quit you must resist, suggestions and temptation to let go. Resist stoutly the negative messages, prophecies and advice from friends and foes alike.

To successfully resist you must re-organize yourself and your priorities. Constantly reorganise and recharge yourself for greater effectiveness. Don't allow things to lie fallow for too long. Reorganize and recheck your schedule and time. Weed out the non-essentials and place your priorities right.

Share:

Selfish people hardly amount to anything in the estimation of men. Stinginess and self-seeking are negative virtues you must avoid as a plague. Get ready to share and serve others. Share your knowledge, time, money, gift and talents with others.

When you share with others, they will inturn share with you. You cannot live alone. To be remembered in life, you must be unselfish with what the Lord had graciously given to you. You must pour out yourself in the service of others. When you are out to serve and share, it is amazing how people will be ready to serve and share with you in return.

Training:

You will need to take the training that will enable you to be effective in your chosen endeavour. Specialized training is available in almost every field of endeavour. Take time and find out these trainings. They will greatly help your self-development.

Simultaneously, trade off your knowledge with others. Train and mobilize your people for active participation in the church. The place and role of training cannot be over-emphasised in the church. Training communicates love, acceptance, care and concern to your people.

> **The key to success is to plan purposefully, prepare prayerfully, proceed positively and pursue perseveringly**

Unction:

Church growth is possible with the anointing of the Holy Spirit. You must receive the unction to function in your divine assignment.

The unction of the Holy Spirit is the non-negotiable requirement for growth in the church. The anointing of the Spirit will result in supernatural growth of the church. This unction cannot fall down like a ripe pawpaw from the sky without much effort in prayer and fasting.

The difference between effective and ineffective ministry is the unction of the Holy Spirit. It must be gotten through consistent fellowship and communion with the Holy Spirit. He is the Spirit of growth and increase.

Every other gimmick, method, tactics and machinery will fail to ignite the fire of revival in the church when the anointing of the Holy Spirit is missing.

Vision:

Vision is the delivery of divine assignment, called ministry. Vision is the bedrock of unquantifiable success in the ministry. You must acquire and imbibe God's vision for your life and church.

Your vision will propel you to success. Your vision will serve as your filter in making decision. You are what you visualize and see. The clear mental image you continually see is what will come to reality. Vision of a better and preferable future must never die in your heart if you are going to make a headway in life.

Warfare, Work:

Working very hard without warfare will still bring little growth in the church. To see growth and breakthrough we must not only work hard, we must work smart. And one of the ways to work smartly is to be engaged in warfare.

> Vision of a better and preferable future must never die in your heart if you are going to make a headway in life

Warfare deals with spiritual powers, strongmen, spiritual wickedness in high places that effectively hinder the growth of churches. Demonic agents inside and outside the church must be defeated and decapacitated if growth must occur.

Without warfare, the church will move at timid and slow pace. It will not have more than a token presence in the community. However, we can win this invisible war. We have the authority and power to deal with these fiendish forces. Yes, we can overcome them and march on to great growth.

X-ray:

It is very necessary for you to periodically x-ray your efforts and activities. Look over your work with the eyes of God and see where there is need for change.

Analyse your programmes as to evaluate their impact and success. Do the stocktaking of all your investments of energy, time, money and outreach in order to discover room for possible change of strategy and refocusing.

X-ray your motives and desires, check up your heart so that you don't allow bitterness, unforgiving spirit and animosity to have control of it. Knowing that if they do, then you can kiss success goodbye.

Yield:

You must have done this first and foremost. Then you continually yield yourself totally, completely and unreservedly unto the Lord.

Give up everything into His hand and surrender everything to Him. Devote and dedicate all you have to Him. Let Him have unhindered reign in your life.

Conversely, yield yourself totally to the fulfillment of your vision. Devote all your energy to bringing your dream of growth into reality. Yes, it can be done, but it will take complete yieldedness and surrenderness.

Zip, Zero:

After you must have prayed, persevered, resisted the enemy, possessed the vision, acquired the anointing, x-rayed your motives and efforts and have now completely yielded to God and your desire for success is deep and you are ready to dare, zip it up and zero in for the kill. Go for it. Don't delay nor waste time.

Now is the time for growth. No other time can be as now. Go for the ripe harvest today. Be like the hunter who shoots not for mere game, but to kill and have result.

Pastors, leaders and ministers, here I rest my case. It is now left for you to do all that God is enabling you in order to see growth in your church. God wants your church to grow.

The Holy Spirit is the Spirit of growth and He is here now to help the growth of your church. So, what are you waiting for? Get into the action for growth!.

International Church Growth Ministries

INTERNATIONAL CHURCH GROWTH MINISTRIES was founded in 1994. The vision of the ministry is to provide current and reliable Church Growth principles in African context to Leaders, Pastors and Ministers that will lead to better and faster growth of their churches.

We do these through books, materials, VCD and audio cassettes at relatively low cost to people engaged in leading the church.

We equally organise seminars and conferences on various aspect of Church Growth and Health. We also accept invitations from churches to help analyse them, motivate their people and generally help the growth potentials of churches.

So far we have ministered to over 20,000 Pastors and Christian Workers across many denominational lines and independent churches. The results have been tremendous and the testimonies have been wonderful and interesting.

The ministry also saw the need to really raise the growth consciousness in the Continent and decided to pioneer an Institute on Church Growth. The response has been overwhelming as so many Pastors, General Overseers, and Church Leaders have enrolled to learn more about how to practically lead their churches to growth. The impact of the Institute on these Pastors' lives have started manifesting in the phenomenal growth of their churches and expansion of their ministries.

ICGM Resources

If you found this book to be useful, you may be interested in some of the other resources available from ICGM.

Listed below are some of our books and resources:

Books:
1. 32 Strategic Ways to Increase Church attendance
2. The Supernatural Leader
3. Your Growth is Your Future
4. The Secrets of Financially Strong Churches
5. Our Churches and His Church
6. Why Churches Breakaway & Lose members
7. Strategic Living
8. Leading Your Church to Lasting Growth
9. 22 Dynamic Laws of Church Growth
10. Strategic Church Planting Today

11. How to Support and Strengthen Your Pastors
12. Leading From the Pulpit
13. Spiritual Warfare for Dynamic Church Growth
14. The Place of Anointing and Administration
15. Family Growth
66. Prayer Nugget
17. Church Growth
18. Financial Growth
19. The Impact Driven Church
20. Grow the Pastor, Grow the Church
21. Personal Growth Today
22. The Loyal Associate

Resources:
a. Spiritual Warfare for church growth
b. Helping the clergy - leading your church to growth.
c. Practical church planting
d. Winning the society seminar
e. Mobilizing the laity
f. Warfare prayer for Growth
g. Closing the Backdoor of the church
h. Women ministry in church growth
i. Strategic level prayer for breakthrough
j. Signs and Wonders for church growth
k. Research and analysing of the church
l. How to grow a vibrant and Healthy churches
m. Why Churches Lose Members
n. Empowering the Church for 21st Century
o. Healthy Leadership for Healthy Churches

p. Tools for Tremendous and Transforming Ministry.
q. New Waves of God's Move for End Time Harvest
r. Magnetic, Multiplying, Marketable and Maximum Impact.
s. Building a Bigger, Better and Broader Church and many others.

Audio Tapes & VCD
1. Spiritual Warfare Series
2. Effective Ministers Series
3. Women Ministry Series
4. Closing the Backdoor Series
5. Warfare Prayer Series
6. Strategic Level Prayer Series
7. Church Planting Series
8. Healthy Church Series.

Journal:
Church Growth Journal is a quarterly teaching and news magazine that gives vital and practical information on how to grow the church.

For further information on these and other resources available, please write or contact us at our office or call the telephone lines provided in this book.

SECRETS OF FINANCIALLY STRONG CHURCHES
By: Francis Bola Akin-John

Do you still have problem raising money to effectively run your ministry or church? Or do you lack proper knowledge on how to manage it to achieve financial freedom for the church? Then this book is for you. It answers your questions about money, tells you why people give or don't give in your church and also offers practical solution to grow a debt - free and financially robust ministry. A must for you if you passionately desire financial buoyancy for your church.

22 DYNAMIC LAWS OF CHURCH GROWTH
By: Francis Bola Akin-John

Church growth is not a logical programme. It is a dynamic process made possible by strict adherence to various laws that guide durable, lasting and solid growth in the church. Violating any of these laws will cause retrogression and stagnation in the church, but an understanding of the laws enumerated in this well researched book will not only ensure growth in your church but it will also sustain the growth in any season. This book is a classic work and still one of the best materials from Africa's foremost Church Growth and Ministerial Consultant, by Francis Bola Akin-John.

YOUR GROWTH IS YOUR FUTURE
By: Francis Bola Akin-John

Growth has no alternative. It is not optional. Your growth is your vehicle to the future. Your growth determines the level you will get to in life. If you desire success passionately either as a pastor, businessman or woman, student, corporate leader, trader, church worker, professional, house wife or church leader, this book is for you. Your personal growth precedes every other growth. Without growth you will become a person of yesterday, abort your greater future and open door for decay. This is a book for everybody.

HOW TO SUPPORT AND STRENGTHEN YOUR PASTOR
By: Francis Bola Akin-John

No church can grow and experience all round increase without the faithful and collective contributions of her members. Unfortunately, many Christians know next to nothing about how to uphold and support their pastors. Here, the author spells out the responsibilities of every church member, associate leaders and heads of various church departments to their pastor - knowing fully well that what makes a good pastor is often the support of good people around him.

32 STRATEGIC WAYS TO INCREASE CHURCH ATTENDANCE
By: Francis Bola Akin-John

Church growth isn't automatic! It is achieved through the combination of spiritual, physical and environmental factors. By indepth research, coupled with rich personal experience as a pastor for many years, Dr. Akin-John highlights diverse strategies for numerical increase and growth in the church. If you read this book and prayerfully implement its content, you will discover that strategy is always better than energy. Get this book if you desire a passionate increase in your attendance. A must for every pastor!

STRATEGIC CHURCH PLANTING TODAY
By: Francis Bola Akin-John

The last two decade witnessed an unprecedented church planting efforts by various Christian denominations, mission- minded individuals and independent ministers. In this book, Dr. Akin-John, himself a researcher on church and ministerial matters, chronicles these efforts and examines the need, method, cost implication, the passion, the benefits, mistakes, misconception, planning, timing, impact, location, the message and the messenger of church planting today. No one has approached church planting than the way this book has done. It is a vintage material from a vintage author.

SPIRITUAL WARFARE FOR DYNAMIC CHURCH GROWTH
By: Francis Bola Akin-John

Achieving outstanding growth in your church is determined by how sharp your attacking instruments of warfare are. The war for control over the territory where your church is located must start in the spirit and end in the spirit. To have peace in your life, family and ministry, you must prepare for war. You must enforce growth and increase by violence in the spirit through all levels of spiritual warfare. Dr. Bola Akin-John made the subject matter more practical than theory here, with strong warning that harvest will tarry in your church unless you are willing to go all out against the visible and invisible powers of the enemy.

OUR CHURCHES AND HIS CHURCH
By: Francis Bola Akin-John

This book is an attempt to put a hand on the crisis that has engulfed the church today. Many practices, methods and models have clearly shown that our 'churches' are not necessarily His church. Many of what we call 'church' today are too far from what Christ had in mind when He said; "I will build my church ". Likewise, many of the people in 'churches' today cannot be said to be His people simply because majority of them do not really know Him. Therefore, if you are really concerned about building His church, and you want to do a work that will not get burnt up, this book is for you! Every Senior Pastor, Bishop, General Overseer and Pastor must read this book over and over again and change where necessary.

LEADING YOUR CHURCH TO LASTING GROWTH
By: Francis Bola Akin-John

Much more than the influx of people into your church and the excitement of ministering to a large crowd, this book unfolds to you powerful strategies necessary to sustain the growth.
Dr. Akin-John goes further to share with you time and field tested biblical principles that will ensure lasting growth and increase in your church.

ICGM Resources

THE PLACE OF ANOINTING AND ADMINISTRATION IN CHURCH GROWTH
By: Francis Bola Akin-John

The sustainable growth of the church of Christ have been gravely affected by wrong notions on the dual issue of Anointing and Administration. It has been discovered that there is lack of balance in the church as regards each of these two areas.
The principles highlighted in this wonderful book provide the needed balanced approach on the issue of Anointing and Administration.
Read it for your edification and practise it for your promotion.

WHY CHURCHES BREAKAWAY AND LOSE MEMBERS
By: Francis Bola Akin-John

The rate at which churches breakaway is almost the same rate churches are being planted. The problem has grown to endemic proportions in the last couple of years, affecting every church either old or new. As a foremost Consultant on ministry and church matters, the author examines the causes of breakaway and membership loses in churches and proffers lasting solutions that will arrest chaos, retrogression, split and membership loses. This is a book every church Founder, General Overseer, Apostle, Superintendent, State and Regional Pastor, Senior Pastor and whoever intends to start a fresh work should read.

PERSONAL GROWTH TODAY
By: Francis Bola akin-John

Dr. Francis Bola Akin-John in this book revealed that the gap between a person's vision and present reality can only be filled through commitment to his personal development. And that personal growth prevents personal and professional stagnation, and surely impacts organisational growth. If you want to reach the height of your potential, personally and professionally, then commit yourself to daily personal improvement.
Personal Growth Today is a classic that must not be missed. Read, study and digest this book over and over again. Drink deep from it and let it become part and parcel of your daily living.

OUR CHURCHES AND HIS CHURCH
By: Francis Bola Akin-John

This book is an attempt to put a hand on the crisis that has engulfed the church today. Many practices, methods and models have clearly shown that our 'churches' are not necessarily His church. Many of what we call 'church' today are too far from what Christ had in mind when He said; "I will build my church ". Likewise, many of the people in 'churches' today cannot be said to be His people simply because majority of them do not really know Him. Therefore, if you are really concerned about building His church, and you want to do a work that will not get burnt up, this book is for you! Every Senior Pastor, Bishop, General Overseer and Pastor must read this book over and over again and change where necessary.

THE LOYAL ASSOCIATE
By: Francis Bola Akin-John

This book is Dr. Francis bola Akin-John humble effort at establishing a right type of relationship between the leader and his associates, providing the right atmosphere for it and bringing sanity into the ungodly madness of unfaithful, disloyal and undependable associates.
It is appropriate for topmost leaders, useful and insightful for those in the middle leadership and challenging to those at the lowest rung of the ladder. If you can adapt and adjust to the timely truth of this book, you will save yourself from many hurts and heartaches.

FRUITFUL AND FULFILLING MINISTRY TODAY
By: Francis Bola akin-John

This book is a tool that will help your ministry to move to the next level. Your ministry is the vehicle you are driving, you need tools to keep it running effectively and fast.
The quickness and durability of your ministry is determined by the tools of ministry at your disposal. Tools will help you to be effective, result oriented, impactful, creative, fruitful and to have tremendous and transforming ministry.
Those tools are scattered throughout in this book. Grab the ones you need by reading, studying, digesting and practising the insights in the book, so that you will no longer work as fools. It is only fools that lack real, genuine, relevant and creative tools for life and ministry.

SEXUAL PURITY IN LEADERSHIP
Dr. Francis Bola Akin-John

Either you like it or not, you will come across sexual pressure in your life and leadership. Leaders that are too simple, innocent and ignorant of the ravages of sexual pressure will surely fall into this trap of the enemy. Many great evangelists, preachers, pastors, bishops and church leaders have lost their anointing and ministry on the laps of strange women.
Sexual Purity in Leadership by Dr. Francis Bola Akin-John exposes the destructive and deadly sexual traps employ by satan against leaders and ministers of God and provides ways to avoid them.
It is a must read for every success-minded leader.

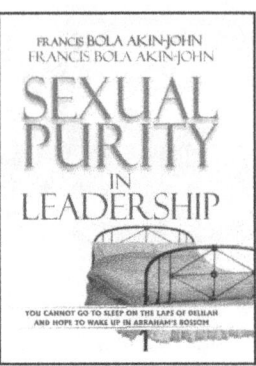

SUPERNATURAL POWER, MIRACLES, SIGNS & WONDERS TODAY
Dr. Francis Bola Akin-John

Many of the great growth of churches today are closely linked with the supernatural dimension of God. Without doubt, these are the days of God's power like never before. Every church and leader must key in to the supernatural move of God, if true and lasting church growth is to be seen and experienced.
This book by dr. Francis Bola Akin-John re-establishes the truth that every church leader can and should display the power of God's kingdom over that of the enemy.
Church leaders and ministers that really desire to operate in the supernatural realm of God must not only read, but also digest, study and soak up this book.

www.ingramcontent.com/pod-product-compliance
Lightning Source LLC
Chambersburg PA
CBHW051753040426
42446CB00007B/345